Towards A Liberal Catholicism

Towards A Liberal Catholicism

Psychology and Four Women

Peter C. Morea

SCM PRESS

0 334 02802 7

This edition first published 2000
by SCM Press
9–17 St Albans Place, London N1 0NX

SCM Press is a division of
SCM-Canterbury Press Ltd

Printed in Great Britain by
Biddles Ltd, Guildford and King's Lynn

For Sally

Acknowledgments

The author wishes, with thanks, to acknowledge permissions for use of quotations from the following works in copyright:

From *Story of a Soul*, translated by John Clarke, OCD. Copyright © 1975, 1976, 1996 by Washington Province of Discalced Carmelites Friars, Inc, ICS Publications, 2131 Lincoln Road NE, Washington, DC 20002 USA.

From *Catherine of Siena, The Dialogue*, translated by Suzanne Noffke, OP, New York: Paulist Press. Copyright © 1980 by The Missionary Society of St Paul the Apostle in the State of New York. Used by permission of Paulist Press.

Taken from *All Shall be Well* by Sheila Upjohn, published and copyright 1992 by Darton, Longman and Todd Ltd and used by permission of the publishers; taken from *The Little Way* by Bernard Bro, published and copyright 1997 by Darton, Longman and Todd Ltd and used by permission of the publishers.

From *Waiting on God* by Simone Weil, translated by Emma Craufurd, copyright 1951, Routledge Ltd, and used by permission of Routledge Ltd; from *Gravity and Grace* by Simone Weil, translated by Emma Craufurd, copyright 1952, Routledge Ltd, and used by permission of Routledge Ltd.

Contents

Introduction

And our soul, by its nature, is rooted in God in endless love.
(Julian of Norwich, *Revelations of Divine Love*)

Truly, You are a hidden God.

(Isaiah 45.15)

Thank her that she has kept the faith for so many generations and do your part in helping her to transmit it to generations after you.
(Cardinal Newman on the church, *The Idea of a University*)

In a scenario from science fiction, astronauts return from civilizations in space seeing themselves and life on earth differently. Without leaving the earth, or the church, Roman Catholics can acquire a different perspective on Catholicism through the insights of psychology and four women. Such insights increase our understanding of Catholicism with regard to our own personality, God, the institutional church and our relationships with other people.

Julian of Norwich, the medieval mystic, was puzzled by a contrast between a compassionate God who never blames and a church judging us as sinners sometimes deserving of anger and blame. Can psychology account for this contrast? Is psychology able to explain why some Catholics believe in Julian's loving and compassionate God, while other Catholics subscribe to a harsher, more negative God? Psychological explanations reveal much about human personality and move us to a more understanding and positive view of others – and ourselves. Psychology might also suggest how we might arrive at Julian's wholly positive view of God.

A tradition has existed in the Roman Catholic Church from which have come barbarous Crusades and Inquisitions; can psychology help explain the cause of this tradition? Can psychology account for the institutional church's long history of often violent antisemitism? Is psychology able to suggest why Catholicism has been so hostile to other branches of Christianity and to other religions, as well as to democracy, freedom of conscience and free intellectual enquiry? Can psychology provide insights about the emergence, within the church, of a preoccupation with sexuality and celibacy, of patriarchy and of certain attitudes to women?

An alternative tradition exists within Catholicism which values equally all human beings, and which stresses the centrality of love and relationships. Psychology provides understanding of how to develop this more liberal Catholic tradition. Psychological awareness helps in our relationships with other people and is relevant to our need for others, and for community, on the journey to God. Psychological understanding of personality and of personality development complements Catholic knowledge of spiritual growth. Psychology, for example, recognizes the importance of the feminine in personal development and of Mary in Catholicism.

Many Catholics regard the significance of Mary as solely religious. For Roman Catholics, devotion to the Virgin expresses a religious truth about God becoming human in Christ and about Mary as the woman who intercedes for us. But the truths of religion may fulfil more than one function. Psychologists see devotion to Mary as satisfying men's need to relate to the feminine in themselves, particularly important with a celibate clergy.

The reality and religious importance of Mary is not explained away, nor diminished, by considering her psychological significance, just as light is not made any less real by the physicist's explanation of light. The explanations of scientific psychology do not supplant Catholicism's religious accounts but supplement them. Psychology extends our understanding of the beliefs and practices of Catholicism by exploring their human dimension. Existential psychology is at one with Catholicism in recognizing our desire to transcend ordinary human experience; but psychology recognizes the powerful reality of our bodily wants and our psychological needs, such as for human love, intimacy and connectedness with others, meaningful sexual relationships, a sense of identity, personal wholeness. Psychology also reveals that what is elevated and holy within Catholicism often mingles with more earthy realities such as pride, aggression, envy, raw sexuality, fear, power.

As a psychologist who is a Roman Catholic, I realize how interconnected in the church are the psychological and the spiritual. Since the secular and the sacred are so interrelated in Catholicism, psychology's insights into the human dimension in the institutional church, its teachings and practices, are of considerable value. If Mary is psychologically important in enabling men relate to their feminine side, modern psychologists also regard, more ambivalently, devotion to Mary as telling women that their place is in the home or convent, and not in the structure and mind of the church.

But the voice of women needs to supplement that of psychology. In this book the understanding of psychology is augmented by the voices of four women in the Christian tradition. They are Julian of Norwich, Catherine of Siena, Thérèse of Lisieux and Simone Weil; each has much to say of relevance to the mysteries of personality, human relationships, God and the church. Any understanding of these mysteries is limited by the limits of our minds; but these minds need not be only those of men.

Julian of Norwich was born in 1342 and died some time after 1416. Part of her life was lived within the city of Norwich, in a cell attached to the church of St Julian, and she probably took her name from the church. In 1373, during a serious illness, she received revelations about the love of God. She seems to have noted down the experiences shortly afterwards and, years later, wrote a longer account of these *Revelations* and her reflections on them. It was probably as a result of her experiences that she became a 'recluse', living alone in a cell built in the wall of the church. Her life would have been one of prayer, though she may have counselled people. The *Revelations of Divine Love* is a deeply spiritual text, scholarly and profound in its theology. Historians regard her as the first woman of letters in England, and she has been described as one of the greatest English theologians; she was the first major theologian to write not in Latin or Greek but in the emerging language that came to be known as English, and probably the first woman to have written a book in English, and in prose of remarkable power.

Though she described herself as uneducated, her writings have considerably influenced Christian thought, and their presence remains pervasive even to the present day, as in the poetry of T.S.Eliot. Julian is a psychologist, insightful about alienation from God, guilt and anxiety, and she anticipates psychologists like Jung in stressing God's maternal side. She emphasizes over and over again God's great compassion and love for humanity; her view of human destiny is one of great optimism. In the *Revelations of Divine Love* Julian is assured by Christ: 'All shall be well, and you shall see for yourself that all manner of thing shall be well.'[1] An abridged version of the *Revelations* in modern English, titled *All Shall be Well*, is used in the following text; Julian quotations are taken from this abridged version, and details on most quotations from the four women are provided in the Notes.

Catherine of Siena, born in 1347, was unusual in exerting influence in the male world of the Roman Catholic Church, even though its hierarchical structure then, as now, was closed to women. The medieval papacy was, at the time, involved in violent conflict with secular governments and had itself split into opposing camps and popes. In spite of pressure from her family, Catherine was determined not to marry, and after a period of prayer she became a member of a group of women affiliated to the Dominican Order. They lived prayerful lives, and Catherine's love of God found expression in the group's work of caring for the poor and sick. Her thought, in part the result of mystical experience, is contained in the *Dialogue*, written as a conversation between her soul and God. For Catherine, God is truth as well as love, and our lives are a search for both. Catherine contrasts our dependent human existence with the absolute being of God; nevertheless this God, she says, desires and needs our love. She sees the importance of both knowledge of God and of self-knowledge on our way to God. Catherine stresses that there are many different paths to God.

Distressed by the church's need for reform and the papacy's corruption, Catherine became much involved in political affairs of church and state. Ignoring the conventions of her time with regard to the subordinate position of women in the church – Christ is reported to have told her, 'In my eyes there is neither male nor female' – she preached and attempted to make popes and cardinals reform, but with little success. She used her influence in an attempt to resolve the papacy's external conflicts with the state and to bring accord to the papacy's internal divisions. Here too most of her work came to nothing; but the role she played was revolutionary for a woman in the Roman Catholic Church in the fourteenth – and twentieth – century. She died in 1380 at the age of thirty-three; she was canonized a saint in 1461. In 1970 she was proclaimed a Doctor of the Roman Catholic Church.

Thérèse Martin was born into a middle-class French family in 1873. Her mother died when Thérèse was four, and her father later suffered from a paralysis which confined him for a time to mental hospital. Thérèse entered a convent at Lisieux in Normandy when she was fifteen to become a Carmelite nun, but it seems from her writings and the comments of others that she would really liked to have been a priest. She died nine years later of tuberculosis in 1897, enduring terrible physical suffering during the last eighteen months of her life. Before her final illness she experienced a spiritual desolation which seems at times to have brought her close to despair. But even during this time of intense doubt she strove to find – and sometimes found – peace.

Thérèse died at the age of twenty-four, unknown to the world, having spent her life in an ordinary household and an obscure convent. She did nothing remarkable in the convent, coming to believe that for herself, and for most of us, life involves accepting mundane tasks and trials in a spirit of abandonment to God. She experienced great dryness in prayer and was regarded as a very ordinary nun, though noted for her sense of humour. But other nuns did eventually realize that there was an extraordinary quality about her ordinariness. At the instruction of her superior, she wrote an account of her life that came to be called *Story of a Soul*. In these autobiographical manuscripts, written in a simple style which does not appeal to everyone, she outlines her thought. For Thérèse, God's relationship with us is one of mercy and love; and Thérèse stressed, like Catherine, the variety of paths and different ways to God. Thérèse had an existential sense of her own nothingness; she experienced life as a condition of exile ending only when we see God. An uneducated woman of immense potential, obedient on the surface but subversive underneath, she speaks for ordinary people. She longs for a fulfilling love. When she is down she gets up with a smile and a joke, but there are tears in her eyes, and – like the rest of us – she has no alternative but to go on. In 1925 Thérèse was canonized a saint, and in 1997 she was made a Doctor of the church.

Simone Weil was French, born in Paris in 1909 into a cultivated agnostic Jewish family. Though eventually coming to regard herself as a Christian, she chose not to be baptized. She disliked the hostility of the Roman Catholic Church – the only Christian church with which she was familiar – to other religious faiths. Simone saw the Catholic Church as very wrong in having ignored so much of value in other faiths and in denying the great truths expressed in other religions. Acutely aware of the dangers inherent in all social organizations, especially for people seeking the good and true wherever they are to be found, she believed her vocation required her to remain outside the institutional church. She saw herself as an outsider and as one speaking for those on the margin. In 1942 she came to England, where she served the French provisional government in exile, and died the following year. It is thought she may eventually have accepted baptism shortly before her death, when she would have known that her contribution as an outsider was ending.

Simone Weil starts from the experience, shared by many, of God's apparent absence from the world – Isaiah's 'Truly, You are a hidden God'. She recognizes that the presence of a loving God is not apparent in the material world, and that modern science describes a universe of physical laws indifferent to human beings. Simone recognizes the paradox of valuing the material world, though knowing it never satisfies us since God seems so absent, at the same time attempting to discover there signs of a divine presence. She finds a solution in four loves which she regards as an implicit love of God: a love of the beauty and order of the world, a love of religious ceremonies, human friendship, and love of our neighbour. Simone values the love of all humanity implicit in a love of our neighbour; but she holds that now, as never before, an all-embracing and explicit love for all our fellow humans is needed. The originality of her thought and its expression in a variety of books, essays, letters and *pensées*, is astounding. She has been called a twentieth-century Pascal.

The thinking of these four women is relevant to an understanding of ourselves, our relationships with others, the church and how we see God. The present book would better have been written by a woman; two women did read and comment on a late draft. And I am a psychologist. In the search for God, ourselves, meaningful human relationships and a greater understanding of the church, Roman Catholics need to listen to psychology as well as women.

The insights of the four women support a psychological understanding of personality which argues the need for a more insightful liberal Catholicism and moves us to greater compassion for others and ourselves. The four women recognize, as does Christian psychology, how close are the human and divine; and they hold that God is to be experienced in other people, our own self and the material world. Together with a Christian psychology, the four women give insight into what influences, obstructs and helps our personality in the search for God and our own identity. For the Roman Catholic, such a search is made from within the community of the church. But the four women and a Christian psychology both emphasize the personal nature of our search for God, and they recognize our relationship with all human beings as central to our search.

The main concerns of the book are with the quartet of personality, other people, God and the institutional Catholic Church. To make this book more accessible, references are only occasionally cited in the text; a comprehensive list is provided under Sources.

The absence of woman's voice from the institutional church, and largely from the New Testament written by men, has affected the language of the institutional church. The Catholic Church retains gender-exclusive language and usually refers to God as male. Language is not responsible for the masculinity of Catholicism's God but has served to confirm his maleness. I have tried to avoid giving God a gender – except where the God referred to is too obviously male!

I wish to thank Loretto Lynch and Mary Jo Radcliffe for their considerable help with comments and suggestions on the text.

Responsibility for the explanations given and any views expressed are mine.

I

God Made in Our Image

We guess; we clothe Thee, unseen King,
With attributes we deem are meet;
Each in his own imagining
Sets up a shadow in Thy seat.

(Gerard Manley Hopkins, 'Nondum')

God made man in his own image, and man returned the compliment by making God in his.

(Very old joke)

We can never come to the full knowledge of God until we first know our own soul clearly.

(Julian of Norwich, *Revelations of Divine Love*)

The Earth that our astronauts returned to is a planet circling a star called the sun in the Milky Way galaxy. According to astronomers, there are millions of stars in our Milky Way galaxy, and many millions of galaxies. The mind of a God who created such a universe must be beyond human comprehension; but Job in the Old Testament pressed its Creator to explain the deaths of his children. The tone of God's answer to Job seems irrational, bullying, insistent on *his* authority – *his* certainly; this God is macho male. Carl Jung, the psychologist, was unimpressed by Job's God; Jung regarded God in the Book of Job as human projection.

In projection, feelings and thoughts that are mine, but which I refuse to admit as mine, I attribute to someone else. 'I think it's disgusting the way people nowadays are so obsessed with sex'; in projection, this obsession that disgusts me, and which I attribute to other people, is really my own. Projection often elaborates: 'I am not aggressive but they are' might become 'I am not aggressive, they are, and they are persecuting me'. Projection means that the anger and authoritarianism in the Book of Job's God is really in Job's own personality.

A religious interpretation takes the Book of Job's message to be that God is unfathomable and cannot be questioned; God has to be trusted in tragedies like the death of a child. A depth-psychology interpretation says that because of projection, not only Job's God but any account of God is likely to be partly our human projection, revealing more about ourselves than about God. For Jung, the Book of Job is a revelation about the condition of the human soul, exposing how far from wholeness human beings are.

According to Jung, when two and a half thousand years ago the author of the Book of Job projected his and other people's thoughts and feelings on God, human and not divine personality was being revealed. Job's angry, power-obsessed, without-insight God is no God but ourselves and is an account of our own disturbed psychological condition. Jung argued that the solution to our disturbed condition, needed as much now as in Job's time, is psychological and spiritual growth to human wholeness. In *Answer to Job*, written shortly after the Second World War, Jung expressed the view that in Europe, where Christianity has been present two thousand years, our psychological condition has scarcely been touched by the message of Christ.

Another book written in time of war about God and human personality is the *Dialogue* of Catherine of Siena. In the fourteenth century, the papacy was in constant conflict with other Italian states and torn by internal strife. In the *Dialogue*, Catherine's account of God is frequently more positive than Job's, with God often assuring her of great love for human beings. Catherine at times sees God's compassion for human beings as unconditional. Other passages in the *Dialogue* seem less confident of divine love, since sometimes in long replies God angrily stresses the punishment in store for unrepentant sinners. And Catherine's God is much preoccupied with devils, whom he damns with relish. Sometimes he seems self-righteous and full of censure in a manner reminiscent of Job's God. Jungian psychology would eventually suspect that here too projection is involved. Catherine's God expresses views that historians would regard as typical of fourteenth-century Catholicism. Indeed, in the unloving and abusive language which God uses to damn many, including ministers of the church, this God seems a particularly judgmental medieval Christian.

There is further evidence of projection in the *Dialogue*; God frequently insists that, regardless of how much priests have abused their power, civil law should have no jurisdiction over corrupt clergy; this was always a sensitive issue with the medieval papacy. In the *Dialogue* God, referring to corrupt priests and bishops, says: 'Now I repeat that, in spite of all their sins and even if they were worse yet, I do not want any secular powers meddling in the business of punishing them.'[1] Indeed, God threatens to punish state authorities who 'sin' by acting against the clergy. The image of God in the *Dialogue*, and the views and feelings that this God expresses, seem at times partly Catherine's projection.

According to depth psychology, what we project on to others comes not from our conscious mind but from our 'unconscious'. Depth psychologists recognize the existence of a personal unconscious, unique to every personality; this unconscious mind consists of thoughts and memories and desires which we do not admit to and have repressed out of awareness. Catherine's and our own views of God are likely to be distorted especially by the contents of the unconscious part of our personality.

Much of our past personal experience is stored within this unconscious; and these unconscious thoughts, feelings, memories and desires reveal themselves in a variety of ways. A man over-reacts to his manager's criticisms – because of forgotten and unconscious incidents from schooldays when his teachers belittled him. The contents of unconscious mind emerge in dreams. A woman repeatedly dreams of an octopus with its tentacles around her – the memory of an oppressive father. Depth psychology sees personality as resembling an iceberg; the conscious mind is the tip of the iceberg above water, and the mass of ice hidden beneath the surface is the unconscious. These unconscious repressed memories, thoughts, feelings and desires, called complexes, affect us without our being aware. A man feels sad one afternoon. The cause, of which he is not conscious, is the low autumn sun and the smell of damp grass reminding him of his sister's funeral. The angry mixed-up feelings that a woman has about her father affect, without her realizing, relationships with male authority figures such as policemen and the headmaster at her children's school. Depth psychology maintains that her feelings about her father will also affect how she sees God. And the more unconscious such feelings are, the more likely we are to project them on to God.

Psychological understanding of projection does not call in question the reality of the external world. A woman's projection of feelings about her father on to a policeman or headmaster does not make the policeman or headmaster any less real. Psychology's concern with the power of projection says nothing about God's existence but stresses how projection can distort our view of God. A man whose father was excessively ambitious for him might project an unconscious image of his father on to God; as a consequence, he sees God as making impossible demands on him. Depth psychology can explain how personal experiences, such as our relationships with parents, enter personality as unconscious complexes, affecting how we see others – and God. But, according to Jung, we are not only affected by our own unconscious personal experiences; he sees another factor at work.

Jung holds that each of us is powerfully affected by the past experience of the whole human species. The woman dreaming of a strangling octopus might have been bullied by an oppressive father; but behind her personal history is all humanity's collective experience of male authority figures. Jung believed that humans are affected and shaped by the shared experience of all human beings through the ages. He refers to this storehouse of memories, which each of us inherits from the past of the human species, as the collective unconscious.

According to Jung, this collective or universal unconscious, which contains the common psychological experience of human beings, is expressed by means of symbols called 'archetypes'. And Jung maintains that a particularly important archetype within each of us is the 'shadow'. The shadow archetype, part of everyone's psychological inheritance and contained within every person's collective unconscious, explains further elements of Job's and Catherine's God.

Standing in the sun, we cast a shadow, and we cast shadows because we have bodies. In Jungian psychology, the archetypal symbol of the shadow expresses an undeniable reality. The shadow expresses the reality that we have flesh-and-blood bodies with demanding instincts, with powerful passions, with strong needs such as sex, with violent emotions such as anger, with aggressive drives. The shadow is the natural animal and instinctive side of ourselves. Different cultures represent the shadow by means of different symbols, and depth psychology sees Christianity as using the symbols of original sin and the devil. In literature, in the Robert Louis Stevenson novel, the menacing Mr Hyde is the shadow side of the respectable Dr Jekyll. In horror films, Dracula is eventually identified by literally having no shadow; the absence of a shadow demonstrates that Dracula is not human. For Jung, the shadow is central to being human, and acceptance of our own shadow is crucial to becoming a whole person.

Catholicism has given a mixed reception to our flesh-and-blood bodies – in Jungian terms, to human personality having a shadow. A dominant Catholic tradition has taught that, as a consequence of Adam's original sin in the Garden, our bodies are innately inclined to sin and evil. In the *Dialogue*, Catherine's God is rather against the body, and she reports God as commending religious people who 'cannot have enough of suffering'.[2] Catherine occasionally displays in the *Dialogue* an obsession with suffering and pain; she is known to have treated her body harshly, existing for long periods without food. Catholicism has also traditionally held that our innate inclination to sin is encouraged by the activity of the devil. And Catherine's solution, in the *Dialogue*, to what Catholicism calls the 'evil inclinations of the flesh' and 'the temptations of the devil' is to destroy them by prayer and penance. For Jung, this traditional Christian strategy is not the complete answer.

In Jungian psychology, Catholicism's 'evil inclinations of the flesh' resulting from original sin is the shadow within; in Jungian psychology, Catholicism's devil is the unconscious shadow projected out. Where a traditional Catholicism holds that the flesh and the devil have to be suppressed and crushed, Jungian psychology stresses that the energies of the shadow are, potentially, so valuable

for human wholeness that the shadow needs to be acknowledged
and harnessed.

In Jungian psychology, growth to psychological wholeness involves extending the conscious area of personality. If our shadow
and personal complexes remain unconscious, we project them;
consequently our image of God consists partly of our projected
complexes and shadow. Hence the aptness of the Gerard Manley
Hopkins line, 'Sets up a shadow in Thy seat'. But if I become aware
of my own harshness, anger and censoriousness, I will recognize
that the harsh judgmental nature that I attribute to God is an aspect
of myself; as a result, I will cease to see God as harsh, bullying and
judgmental. The greater the extent of my conscious mind, the fewer
negative elements there are in my unconscious for me to project on
to God, and the more positive will be my view of God. But the more
my mind remains unconscious with regard to the shadow, the more
I will project my shadow on to God and the more negative will be
my view of God.

The same process with regard to projection occurs in relation to
people. Depth psychology recognizes the psychological soundness
of Christ's advice about the beam in our own eye and the speck in
our brother's. If I become aware of my own aggressiveness, sexuality, selfishness, envy and can acknowledge them as mine, I will
stop projecting them on to other people.

Twentieth-century novelists, like William Golding, in books
such as *Lord of the Flies*, have emphasized the irrational, violent and
passionate forces within human personality, which Jung terms the
shadow. Jung holds that the power of bodily instinct and aggression
remains always with us; the shadow never surrenders, he says.
Depth psychology recognizes the value of the Christian stress on
will and self-control in life. But Jungian psychology regards the
Christian emphasis on crushing and destroying our shadow side as
misconceived and, as most of us know, it largely proves unsuccessful. The sexually-active lives of some supposedly celibate priests –
in Catherine's time and throughout Catholic history – confirms this.
Jung holds that, by and large, the instinctual shadow side is potentially dangerous only when unconscious, becoming a positive force
for good when acknowledged and admitted to consciousness.

Much modern literature, such as the novels of Hermann Hesse, explores a relationship between negative and positive forces within human personality. The conclusion of Jungian psychology is that while archetypes such as the shadow and psychological complexes remain unconscious, they control us; when they are raised into consciousness, we control them. The solution, according to Jung, is to integrate our unconscious shadow and complexes into our conscious self, where they are transformed into valuable sources of energy. Jung's view is anticipated in the old tale of Beauty and the Beast.

In the story, the shadow side of personality is symbolized by the beast. The beast is undoubtedly sexual both as animal and human prince, and there is a hint of violence in his threat to Beauty's father. Psychologically, the story is saying that a split exists in human beings between the instinctual animal side and higher conscious mind. Wholeness is what humans seek, and in the story the division is ended by the embrace of Beast and Beauty. In Jungian terms, for wholeness we need to acknowledge and accept our instinctual side, to allow our shadow to become conscious. Jung held that when the powerful instinctual forces which the shadow symbolizes are integrated into conscious personality, they are changed into an energy for good – for commitment, creativity and appropriate self-assertion. The Beast is transformed into the Prince by Beauty's kiss; it is being loved which makes the Beast lovable. Conscious personality's kiss and acceptance of the shadow brings more unity to the human person and enables the positive and good nature of the beast within to emerge. Depth psychology, expressing this symbolically, sees a need for the devil not to be banished by God but to be reconciled with God.

Jung maintains that if we acknowledge and accept the shadow as part of ourselves, we take a major step towards making ourselves whole. The unconscious shadow is dangerous and needs to be controlled, but Jungian psychology holds that the instincts and passions symbolized by the shadow are potentially the source of creative energy. Jung described the shadow as '80% gold'. If Dr Jekyll refuses to acknowledge the other side of himself, Mr Hyde becomes a terrible threat. If the split between Jekyll and Hyde within us continues, the unconscious and potentially explosive shadow remains a danger to ourselves and others. But, according to Jung, when the shadow is integrated within personality and becomes part of the self, we have a powerful source of vitality and creative energy and passionate goodness.

But depth psychology recognizes that bringing our shadow and complexes into consciousness is difficult and often the work of a life-time; with many of us the domain of the unconscious remains large throughout our lives. And since whatever is unconscious tends to be projected, there remains always the danger that our view of God is partly projection of our unconscious, as Job's and Catherine's seem partly to have been. Though Catherine's God is much more a God of love than Job's, her God's attitudes to human beings are some-times mixed, often in the *Dialogue* judging sinners harshly and at great length, and often emphasizing the obedience owed to him by humans. The democratic feel of the New Testament, of humans as God's heirs and fellow heirs with Christ, and the promise of their becoming partakers of the divine nature, is sometimes absent from Catherine's *Dialogue*.

Many scholars now agree that Catherine's extraordinary fasts have the characteristics of anorexia nervosa. In her fasting, Catherine might at one level have been motivated by the desire to do penance and to mortify herself. But at an unconscious level there seems to have been an element of self-loathing and of disgust with her own body, typical of people suffering from anorexia. Catherine's possible anorexia and her denigration of herself, in spite of having worked for years among the destitute and tending the sick in time of plague, suggest that she is troubled by unsorted-out shadow within her unconscious. Possibly Catherine's harsh judgmental God is Catherine's own unconscious shadow projected, and her loving compassionate God is the perception of her conscious mind.

But conscious as well as unconscious factors cause negative images of God, and Catherine's God seems at times the creation of a dutiful daughter of a judgmental church. She lived in a time when the institutional church preached that the fate of much of humanity was eternal damnation by God. The medieval church's view of God as so punishing would have influenced Catherine's conscious views. But at an unconscious level also Catherine would probably have been affected by so condemning and damning a church. It seems likely that a harsh and judgmental Catholicism makes more difficult accepting ourselves as we really are, unconscious complexes and shadow included. So it seems likely that in a judgmental church we will be more inclined to project our own shadow and to see God negatively.

The Jungian explanation for a church, consciously holding the idea of a loving God as central to its teaching, but which seems more influenced by a view of God as harsh, is again unconscious shadow. In a Jungian account, the church of Catherine's time, unable to acknowledge its shadow side, projected its own shadow on to God. Jungian psychology would suggest that when the Catholic God is harsh and judgmental, like Job's, the cause is projection of unconscious shadow by the institutional church, and reveals much about the church and nothing about God.

But depth psychology recognizes the influence of personal factors and individual differences. Julian of Norwich, too, lived in the time of a harsh authoritarian church but was able to see God as totally loving. 'In this love without beginning he made us, and in the same love he looks after us, and never allows us to be harmed,'[3] says Julian in the *Revelations of Divine Love*, where she constantly stresses the eternal and unconditional nature of God's love.

And possibly Catherine had some awareness that the judgmental element in her account of God was related in some way to herself. God tells her in the *Dialogue*: 'But know that my mercy toward you is incomparably more than you can see, because your sight is imperfect and limited, and my mercy is perfect and without limit.'[4] Jungian psychology might suggest that Catherine had partly come to terms with her unconscious; as a result, in her overall perception of God she is striving to overcome negative projections from her unconscious. Catherine is reported in a biography to have told Christ that she could never reconcile herself to the thought of anyone being lost to God. And in spite of God's frequent threats of damnation for the disobedient in the *Dialogue*, the dominant message remains God's unconditional love for humanity.

Catherine's *Dialogue* asserts that belief in God's love enables us to become whole, helps us stop judging others and makes us more able to love God and other people. Thérèse of Lisieux, believing in a compassionate God who calls us to a relationship of equality, also holds that the sort of God we believe in influences the sort of person we become. Thérèse, too, saw God's love for human beings as unconditional. She held that in our relationship with God we need to be accepted as we are; and she affirms that God does just that, accepts and loves us as we are. Psychology similarly maintains that, for psychological development, human beings need relationships of unconditional love and acceptance. Psychologists regard both the need and capacity for relationships as part of inborn human nature; research demonstrates that babies, even before they have acquired language, attempt to communicate with others such as their mothers.

But psychology also demonstrates that our capacity for relationships, though innate, has to develop through experience, especially in childhood through the experience of being loved by parents and other adults. Thérèse, similarly, holds that we love God because it is our innate nature to do so, but also because we learn to love God through knowing that we are loved by God. Thérèse reports in her autobiography, *Story of a Soul*, how the experience of God's love for her motivated her to love God in return – 'but He has willed that I KNOW how He has loved me with a love of *unspeakable foresight* in order that now I may love Him unto *folly!*'[5]

But though Thérèse holds to the traditional Catholic view that the person you become is shaped by the sort of God you believe in, she appears at times to be aware of the more psychological view, that the sort of God you believe in is shaped by the sort of person you are. This insight is expressed in a comment that she is reported as having made to a nun insisting on God's justice: 'Sister, if you want divine justice, you will get divine justice. The soul gets exactly what it expects of God' (Bro, *The Little Way*). Thérèse seems to be saying that we might see God as judgmental because, on account of the person that we are, we wish to see God as judgmental. This resembles the Jungian understanding of how our perception of the divine moves from personality to God: if we are full of unconscious anger and judgment, we are likely – in the manner of the *Book of Job*

– to project and to see God as angry and judgmental; if we become whole and loving, we are more likely to see God as loving.

New Testament images of a God of love and compassion, which Thérèse presents continually in her autobiography and Catherine in much of the *Dialogue*, console and fill us with hope. But depth psychology asks whether seeing God consciously in such positive terms significantly improves us. The institutional church's history of intolerance and violence done to others suggests that conscious belief in a God of love seems to have made little difference. The cause, Jung maintains in *Answer to Job*, is that we are largely unchanged at the level of the unconscious; according to Jungian psychology, in spite of two thousand years of Christianity we remain in our unconscious much as Job revealed in his projections on to God – violent, intolerant, authoritarian, psychologically disturbed, lacking in insight.

To the question why Christians have been so little changed by belief in a loving God, Jungian depth psychology answers that we are only minimally affected by the sort of God we believe in consciously. Depth psychology holds that how we think, feel and act, and the sort of God we really subscribe to, is a consequence of the sort of person that we are. And the sort of person that we are, according to depth psychology, is largely a product of the natural forces forming our personality, particularly at the level of the unconscious; in turn, our personality largely shapes our thoughts, feelings and actions, and how we see God and other people.

Psychology suggests that since a significant part of our personality is often unconscious, the God that in practice we subscribe to is largely a product of our projections. If our personality, particularly at an unconscious level, is inclined to be authoritarian, intolerant, dogmatic, then the God we create with our projections will be an authoritarian God who demands unreflecting obedience, punishes and feels no need to give reasons. The God we subscribe to, the God who influences us, is partly the God we make in the image of our own unconscious. The capacity to believe truly in a loving and compassionate God relates to our whole personality, unconscious and conscious.

It is when our own personality is loving, accepting and caring that we are able to believe in the Christian God of compassion and unconditional love. Both Catherine and Thérèse are eventually able to believe in such a God because they come to achieve a certain wholeness and holiness in their lives. But belief in such a God did not come easily for either of them, and we can observe their struggle to see God more positively. Thérèse's development can clearly be discerned, in her autobiography, *Story of a Soul*, as a struggle to achieve wholeness and holiness through recognition and acceptance of herself as she really is.

Jungian depth psychology sees greater awareness of ourself, of our unconscious mind and particularly of the shadow, as crucial to psychological development. Psychology complements the Christian doctrine, that we are made in God's image, with the warning that we are always in danger of making God in our own image and, particularly, in the image of our unconscious shadow. Depth psychology, aware of the extent to which projection interferes with how we see God and others, holds that growth to human wholeness requires the domain of the unconscious to diminish. A Christian psychology stresses, in addition to a traditional Christian emphasis on the power of grace and belief in a loving God, the strength of natural forces in determining our personalities – and how we see God. A Christian psychology, influenced by the insights of depth psychology, maintains that the more personality becomes conscious, the greater is our capacity for love, compassion and concern for others and the less distorted is our perception of other people – and God.

A depth-psychology interpretation suggests that if we have difficulty believing in a loving God, it might be because our perception is distorted by psychological damage to our own personality. And an understanding of Catherine, Thérèse, Julian, Simone Weil and others suggests that the less our view of God is obscured by projection and the unconscious, the more likely each of us is to see God as God really is, loving and compassionate.

2

But for the Grace of God and . . .

The truth, that moral judgments must remain false and hollow, unless they
are checked and enlightened by a perpetual reference to the special circumstances that mark the individual lot.

(George Eliot, *The Mill on the Floss*)

But because of the contradictions in us, we often fall into sin.

(Julian of Norwich, *Revelations of Divine Love*)

You must never pass judgment in human terms on anything you see or hear . . .
there is no one who can judge the hidden heart.

(God speaking to Catherine of Siena, *Dialogue*)

Seeing a drunk in the gutter, a saint is reported to have said: There
go I, but for the grace of God. A modern psychologist is more likely
to say: There go I, but for my biology, my past and my present.
Psychology reveals how our bodies, our past psychological experience (especially in early childhood) and our present social circumstances largely govern our lives. Simone Weil, too, held that human
behaviour is shaped by natural laws in the way that the material
world is determined by physical laws. She refers to these laws
governing personality as 'gravity'. Simone Weil's notion of gravity
is a recognition, in accord with modern psychology, of the reality of
cause and effect in human life. In more ways than one, the drunk is
in the gutter because of gravity.

Freud's psychology emphasizes the influence of biology on
human beings. He regarded the infant as little more than biology
and bodily instinct at birth. His psychoanalytic account recognizes
the importance of mind, consciousness, our capacity for love and
human relationships, but Freud regarded these as developing subsequently in our lives. He stressed the influence throughout our

lives of inborn instincts as sources of energy, desire and pleasure, and as the cause of much of our behaviour. And Freud saw that most of us, finding insufficient the bodily satisfactions which society provides, often feel the pain of frustrated instinct. He held that depression, anxiety, phobias, obsessions, hysteria, paranoia and psychological collapse are partly a product of our inability to tolerate or sublimate frustrated instincts.

A Freudian psychoanalytic account holds that a life instinct motivates our breathing, eating, drinking, defecating and having sex. The life instinct drives the body to seek self-preservation, pleasure, excitement and is the basis of our love for others and of our need for human relationships. But Freud, appalled by the carnage of the First World War, concluded that our bodies are also motivated to move from life to death. The body, weary of the tension of existence, longs to return to the repose of lifeless matter. In the Freudian account, the death instinct, turned against ourselves, leads to depression and self-mutilation, even suicide; directed outwards, the death instinct causes violence, aggression, war.

If we doubt the validity of Freud's emphasis on the power of human instinct, we should observe babies. Babies demand satisfaction of hunger and thirst; they clamour for comfort, dryness, warmth; and they get angry when these needs are not instantly satisfied. Babies demand to be held and caressed and cuddled with a desperation which reveals the power of their need for physical human contact. Freud maintains that whatever else psychologically we are or might become, we remain bodies, and our innate bodily instincts affect us throughout life. Stressing the power of human biology, the Freudian psychoanalytic account makes us, like the psychologist with the drunk in the gutter, less judgmental of others. In contrast, at the Council of Trent in the sixteenth century, the Catholic Church condemned every 'wrong' sexual act, even if it were not genital, as grave sin.

Though, in the Freudian account, our bodies have considerable power over all of us, the psychology of individual differences recognizes how different people are. There appear to be individual variations in the strength of our needs for bodily satisfactions, such as for sex or alcohol, or in the capacity to manage without them. And individuals seem to differ in their ability to live with the tension of frustrated instincts and in the capacity to sublimate them. Such variations may partly relate to our different genetic make-up. There appears to be a biological basis for certain personality differences, such as introversion and extraversion. Introverts are characterized by Jung as cautious and careful people, anxious in new situations. Extraverts tend to act confidently much of the time, usually sure that what they are doing is right. As a result the introvert is likely to be judged a coward – especially by an extravert! The insight that the differences in what we do is often the result of inborn bodily differences might also incline us to be less judgmental of other people.

Freud's psychoanalytic theory, though emphasizing the power of our inborn instincts, recognizes also the importance of past experience. The psychologist, seeing the drunk, maintains that there are causes other than biological differences why we are not in the gutter next to him; we might not be there because our personal histories differ from his. In Freud's view, the past satisfaction and frustration of instincts, particularly in infancy, shape adult life. Like Freud, a great number of psychologists stress the influence of our past, emphasizing the importance of childhood experience.

According to Freud, the focus of the infant's instinctual needs changes through early childhood. At first, mouth and lips and tongue are the chief sources of satisfaction, since there the baby experiences the life-and-death activity of eating and drinking. At this oral stage, the infant experiences its hold on life as linked to the arrival in good time of breasts, bottle or harder foods. Research supports Freudian theory in finding that frustration and gratification in early feeding cause certain personality traits as adults. Depending on whether the pain and pleasure are experienced early or late in this oral stage, we mature into adult personalities inclined either to be passive, pessimistic, gullible and helpless, or to be assertive, cynical, sarcastic and argumentative.

According to Freud, there follows an anal stage from about nine months to the age of four, when the infant is focussed on anus and bowels; these become even more central to the child's experience when parents begin toilet training. Freudian theory again maintains that varying experiences of pleasure, pain and anxiety at this stage result in different personality traits; again research provides some evidence. Children who obtained great satisfaction in the expelling of faeces, or whose parents took a more permissive attitude towards bowel control, are likely to mature into explosive and bossy personalities, who let you know just how they feel and tend to be insensitive to other people's feelings. If parents placed great emphasis on acquiring bowel control, children are likely to grow up orderly and parsimonious, controlling and obstinate adults who have difficulty in coping with change.

Freud states that at the oedipal stage around the age of four or five, the penis and clitoris, though not adult sex organs, become sources of great sensual pleasure – and pain and anxiety. According to Freud, a development of crucial importance now occurs. At the oedipal stage, if psychological growth proceeds satisfactorily, the young child acquires an unconscious conscience. In the Freudian account, the little boy internalizes his father, at the same time taking in father's values; the little girl internalizes her mother, at the same time taking in mother's values: in the process, both acquire the unconscious conscience that Freud calls the super-ego.

What subsequently emerges in puberty, according to the psychoanalytic account, is the genital personality. Freud regards the adult genital personality, characterized by the need and capability for human love and relationships, as the goal towards which the healthily developing child proceeds. Genital personalities are concerned with the needs and pleasures of other people as well as with their own. The genital personality both wants, and has the capacity for, mature loving human relationships. Freud's belief, that the genital personality, able to give and receive love in reciprocal relationships, emerges from healthy early development, underlines the importance of childhood. Similarly, Freud's view that impaired psychological development during those early years causes difficulty with love and relationships in adult life again emphasizes the importance of childhood.

Many psychologists follow Freud in seeing childhood experience as adding to the tyranny that our instinct-driven bodies have over us. Our early history affects the rest of our lives by shaping adult personality. As grown men and women, parts of us remain psychologically infants and affect how we behave. A man who as a child was always expected to take responsibility for his handicapped younger brother may find fatherhood a burden, returning him to the strain that he experienced as a child. Excessive conformity as adults might originate in our parents loving us only if we were obedient and did as we were told. As adult Roman Catholics we might, in our uncritical acceptance of pronouncements from religious authority, still be fearful infants regarding everything that father says as infallible. Alternatively, a woman may be able to question the rulings of the papacy because, as a child, she was certain of her parents' love and was allowed occasionally to challenge them. Freud sees the frustrations of infancy as causing fixation at childhood stages, with the danger in adult life of regressing psychologically to childhood, particularly when our personality is under pressure.

According to Freud, the power of bodily instincts and childhood experience is further increased, and made more irrational, because their influence over us is often unconscious. He held that there exist, within our personal unconscious, instinctual desires and childhood experiences of which we are unaware. We have 'repressed' them because they were too painful, because they created too much guilt, because of their violent or sexual content, or because something else made them unacceptable to our conscious mind. Freud believed that our instincts are never tamed and that the intense experiences of childhood remain with us throughout adult life, the influence of both often being all the greater because unconscious.

Freud, in seeing the genital personality as the goal of human development, emphasizes the importance of relationships in adult life. The practice of Freudian therapy, where the psychoanalyst listens and relates to the client, illustrates the value that Freud places on human relationships. But Erich Fromm goes further. Fromm, a neo-Freudian, maintains that relationships are central to the human adult and crucial to the psychological development of the child; but he holds also that relationships in childhood shape the type of adult personality that we become.

Fromm, like Freud, stresses the influence of childhood experience on our adult life; but what Fromm regards as central to the healthy development and shaping of personality is not biology and instinct but the relationships experienced by the child. What, according to Fromm, causes a child to grow into a passive oral adult is not breast-feeding in itself, but mother's relationship with the child, which emerges in her breast-feeding. The child may have grown into a clinging oral personality, lacking in initiative, also because the parents were domineering, insisted on unquestioning obedience and blocked any initiative. Similarly, it is not toilet-training as such that causes a child to grow into an obsessional and stubborn anal personality, but the relationship with the child that the parents express in the toilet-training. Other experiences could also have caused the child to become an anal adult, such as certain tension in the family, a controlling father, a mother's insistence on caution in trusting others, an anxious elder brother. What, in Fromm's view, shapes children into the type of adult personalities that they become is the sort of relationship they experience with parents, siblings and others.

The development of the child, says Fromm, is related to relationships within the family. And Fromm sees relationships within a particular family as largely shaped by the personalities of parents, by the wider society and by the family's social position within society. Fromm regards relationships with others as the central issue for every human individual. The importance of relationships for human beings is stressed by almost all theories of personality. Similarly, developmental accounts of personality, such as those of Fromm and Erikson, hold that personality grows and develops through loving relationships with other human beings.

W. R. D. Fairbairn even sees adult personality as originating largely in the relationships experienced in childhood. Fairbairn, in his theory of object relations, maintains that our adult lives are governed by our childhood relationships because such relationships actually make us the way we are. Object-relations theory, sometimes referred to as interpersonal-relations theory, sees that human beings seek satisfying personal relationships; indeed, Fairbairn regards the need to love, and to be loved by others, as our strongest human need. And object-relations theory contends that the manner in which our need, to be loved and to love, is satisfied in infancy and childhood constructs personality.

In the object-relations account, humans seek to relate to others, and be related to by others, not as means but as ends. What we really want in relationships is the experience of other people as valuable in themselves, and for ourselves to be experienced by others as valuable in ourselves. For example, in an object-relations account of healthy human sexual behaviour, what is sought in another person is primarily a relationship, with sexual pleasure as the outcome of that relationship. According to Fairbairn, human beings are primarily relationship-seeking, and throughout life satisfying relationships are primarily what humans seek.

Fairbairn maintains that children are born psychologically whole. But children need to have their identity, worth and value confirmed through being loved by others and by having their love accepted by others. Unfortunately, parents' relationships with their children are inevitably less than perfect and provide the child with only a flawed sense of worth and value. Children become anxious when their need to be loved, and to have their love accepted by others, is inadequately satisfied and the wholeness with which they began life fragments. In object-relations terms, the originally whole and unified self splits. The split and fragmented self, emerging from the imperfect relationships of childhood, becomes the basic structure of our personality. This fall from primal and innocent wholeness is evoked every time the middle-aged or elderly tell of how the golden years of their youth gave way to the conflicts of modern society! But for Fairbairn, this 'fall' from grace occurs in the first years, or months, of life.

Fairbairn sees this structure of personality, emerging from childhood relationships, as usually lasting all our lives; changes in later years are achieved only with great difficulty. In a distinction similar to Jungian introversion and extraversion, Fairbairn regards two particular orientations of personality, the schizoid and depressive, as the product of childhood. He sees the schizoid-orientated personality as an adult full of anger and often a cold animosity. Schizoid personalities have difficulty in loving and getting close to people, fearing their closeness will damage those that they love. So schizoid personalities tend to hide behind a mask of superiority, indifference and cynicism; because of this they are judged by others as arrogant and unfeeling. Fairbairn sees the contrasting depressive personalities as adults fearful their anger will hurt those they love. As a result, depressives have difficulty asserting themselves and expressing anger with those whom they love, but they are often irritable and critical with people outside their close circle, such as subordinates at work. So depressives too are judged – for being weak, lacking in moral fibre, obsequious with those close to them, unkind to others. According to Fairbairn, schizoid and depressive personalities, whether in mild or extreme form, are created by the experience of certain kinds of childhood relationships. Object–relations theory supports the view that our different personalities, making us behave as adults in the different ways that we do, are formed in infancy.

Behaviourist psychology, usually referred to as behaviourism, also regards humans as formed by their experience; but the behaviourist account of how this happens differs from that of psychoanalytic tradition. Behaviourism holds that we are born with a handful of needs and emotions, and that subsequently we are variously shaped by positive and negative reinforcement. This behaviourist explanation might seem naïve and simple but has been implicitly adopted by parents throughout history. To make children 'behave', parents have rewarded them; to stop children 'misbehaving', parents have punished them. Research and observational studies confirm that reward such as praise or giving more attention, and punishment such as criticism and ignoring the child, do shape children's behaviour. Studies have demonstrated that positive and negative reinforcement make children behave less disruptively, work harder in the classroom, become more assertive, share their toys more.

According to behaviourism, what parents have not realized is the importance of the way in which reward and punishment is given. Positive and negative reinforcement may be received straightaway or be delayed; one drinker may have a headache immediately after several glasses of wine, and another feel nothing till the following morning. Positive and negative reinforcement may be given regularly like a weekly pay-packet or irregularly like a fruit machine.

Reward and punishment can be given directly or can be received indirectly, as when we observe another person being thanked or blamed. The vicarious experience of seeing other people positively and negatively reinforced powerfully affects us. If children see other children being praised for being tough and assertive, they are likely to imitate them, and they will tend to become tough and assertive themselves.

Behaviourist psychology maintains that we share or are selfish because our sharing or selfish acts have been positively or negatively reinforced in the past. We have learnt to be aggressive or caring because when circumstances made us act aggressively or caringly in the past, we were rewarded. What matters is the pay-off for what we do. What makes us what we are – supportive, dependent, honest, untruthful, kind or cruel – is the positive or negative reinforcement by others, such as by affection or disapproval, giving or withholding of gifts, encouragement or blame. One man is gentle and another tough, one woman is assertive and another timid, as a consequence of past positive and negative reinforcement. Being tender and loving, or being unfeeling and distant, is not something we choose, but what we have been trained and taught to be by past reinforcement. Behaviourists would suggest, and many marriage counsellors would agree, that being a good husband or wife is largely a product of positive and negative reinforcement.

Thérèse of Lisieux is somewhat behaviourist in her emphasis that everyday actions and behaviour are crucial in forming and shaping us. But Thérèse also emphasizes the importance of motivation, insisting that for moral development our everyday actions need to be motivated by love of God and other people. In contrast, behaviourism maintains that we become 'good' or 'bad' simply by acquiring good and bad habits as a result of positive and negative reinforcement: what we are and what we do are the result of the habits that we have formed. The behaviourist psychologist would stress that habits, created by past positive and negative reinforcement, are likely to be the cause of the drunk being in the gutter.

Like behaviourism, social psychology too holds that the experiences which shape us are not confined to childhood. Nevertheless, the social psychology of G.H. Mead's symbolic interactionism does regard our relationships with others in childhood as crucial; indeed, symbolic interactionism contends that the self (in Mead's use of the term) emerges from interaction with other people in our earliest years. The making of the self begins when infants imitate the actions of others, meaninglessly at first, then later with some understanding; through such imitation, infants learn to play the parts of people important to them, such as parents, siblings and others. By acting the roles of these *significant others*, infants and children acquire an awareness of what people expect of them. Eventually children develop core selfs and identities to cope in a more generalized way with the common expectations which other people have of them. A self emerges to meet the expectations of this composite of significant others, called a *generalized other*. Symbolic interactionism maintains that the selfs of human beings usually have much in common because they emerge from certain common expectations. But Mead also holds that since significant others differ for each child, each child's generalized other and what is expected of each child will be different. As a result, the self acquired in childhood varies from individual to individual.

According to symbolic interactionism, our self (in the Meadian sense) is essentially created by our relationships with others in childhood; but Mead stresses that even in adult life our self is maintained by the people and society around us. Social psychology holds that we require society and human relationships to enable our identity to continue existing; our self is sustained throughout adulthood by interaction with others. We continue to be shaped, even as adults, by the relationships that surround us in society, and particularly by relationships important to us.

A young Catholic, feeling called by Christ to serve others and particularly the vulnerable, enters a seminary to become a priest. In the years that follow, as curate and parish priest and finally as a bishop, he is surrounded and influenced by fellow-members of the Catholic Church. He eventually internalizes the view of those around him, that what matters above all is the church, since only if the institution remains strong can the church serve others. His self has become so identified with the organization that the church's survival and growth is now seen by him as paramount. Without realizing, his original reason for entering the priesthood, which was the service of others, has become secondary to the survival and prestige of the organization. As bishop, and faced with a priest in relationship with a woman, his main concern is to avoid damage to the church by keeping the affair concealed, ending the relationship and moving the priest to another parish. His original reason for becoming a priest, the service of others and particularly of the vulnerable – here the woman and any children – has been changed by his life within the institutional church. In the social psychology account, even when we are adults, relationships with other people continue to shape our self and our actions.

However, social psychology and behaviourism also maintain that personality and behaviour are shaped not only by recent adult experience and distant past infancy, but also by immediate circumstances. Both social psychology and behaviourism see our actions as formed by the present daily social situation. Whether we are aggressive, docile, competitive or co-operative is partly the result of circumstances now. Some people are competitive at work and non-competitive in the pub. Some people are entertaining and noisy at home, serious on the sports field, shy and quiet at work. Someone in a crowd behaving violently in a way that is normally untypical of him dramatically illustrates the influence of immediate circumstances. Both behaviourist and social psychologists emphasize the power over us of contemporary circumstances.

So, in a social psychology account, human personality is not only created by human relationships but also depends for its continuing survival on present relationships and circumstances. The man in the gutter may have become a drunk because his marriage is under strain, and his marriage may be under strain because he has been made redundant through no fault of his own. 'Our personality is entirely dependent on external circumstances which have unlimited power to crush it,'[1] says Simone Weil in *Waiting on God*.

Social psychology emphasizes that it is not only our behaviour that society shapes; we are socialized by society into holding certain views, beliefs and values. At every moment we are influenced by those around us and tend to acquire the current attitudes and prejudices of our society and culture. Social psychology likens our social situation to acting in a play, as Shakespeare does: 'All the world's a stage, And all the men and women merely players.' If we disagree with society's account of our part in the play and with society's expectations about what we should think, pressures will be applied such as ridicule, persuasion and shame, and in the last resort, force. But where no alternatives exist to society's values, views and ideas, we usually accept them as correct and believe that they are right and true.

The Catholic Church has always been aware of society's power to determine what we believe, particularly when no alternative beliefs are available. From early in church history until modern times, the Catholic Church has persecuted Jews. In the past, one cause of the church's antisemitism, especially during the Middle Ages and Renaissance, was that the continuing presence of devout Jews in Europe demonstrated the reality of religious faiths other than Catholicism. The presence of practising Jews revealed the possibility of holding beliefs different from the beliefs of Catholics, which the church contended were the only true beliefs. Even in modern times, the institutional church has preferred to operate in situations where only its own teachings are available. As late as 1864, Pope Pius IX asserted in his *Syllabus of the Principal Errors of Our Time* that Catholicism should continue as the only religion of a country to the exclusion of all other ways of worship. An authoritarian church operated on the principle that the absence of beliefs at variance with church dogma made it more likely that church teaching would be accepted without any questioning.

But social psychology sees the power of society extending beyond forming what we do, think and believe; society eventually enters each of us to make us what we are and to create our identity. A boy is brought up by Catholic parents who feel a certain guilt about sex; he goes to primary school where he is taught by nuns who regard the body and bodily functions with a certain distaste; as an adolescent, among his teachers are priests whose lives suggest the inferiority of sexuality to celibacy; as a young male he masturbates and is told in confession of the sinfulness of what he does. Social psychology maintains that the passing of time, and his years of married life, do not make irrelevant this past conditioning in respect of sex. A social psychological understanding emphasizes that this past social learning, once external to him, is now within him and forms part of his very self. Guilt, shame and anxiety in relation to body and sexuality, present while his identity was formed by his Catholic environment, have become an element in the adult self which he now is. Social psychology recognizes that such guilt, shame and anxiety cannot be sloughed off like a dead skin, because they are not skin but are part of his core identity.

Social psychology sees the human self as developing out of our relationships as children and adults. We stop acting the parts we are playing in society and become them. As adults, we are the parts that society and other people assign us. What was originally only in society is internalized and is now in me . . . is me. This self of mine which I experience as uniquely me is largely the creation of society. If I am aggressive or timid, a domineering or passive person, this is partly the product of society's expectations of me. Similarly, social psychology suggests that if a man, as bishop or pope, is surrounded daily by subordinates who consider his authority to be almost absolute, he may end up believing himself to be possessed of some special power. As a result, he might come eventually, through no fault of his own, to hold that he is always right and his every word should be obeyed.

No religious thinker was more aware than Simone Weil of the power that the social, in the form of society and organizations and institutions, has over us. She writes of the social being the domain of the devil. She observed that a collective, such as the church, takes on a transcending authority in relation to the individual; and Simone recognized that before such apparently sacrosanct authority the individual conscience is, at times, almost powerless. She saw the individual as often deceived and led astray by the social.

Psychology stresses the extent to which human actions are caused by natural forces, and Simone Weil with her notion of gravity aligns herself with modern psychology. She sees 'gravity' as laws at work within personality, controlling what we do in a cause-and-effect way, like natural forces determining the workings of the material world. She believes that only God's grace can liberate us from the awesome power of this gravity. In *Gravity and Grace*, Simone writes: 'All the *natural* movements of the soul are controlled by laws analogous to those of physical gravity. Grace is the only exception.'[2]

Catholicism stresses the importance of grace. Though individual Catholic thinkers have recognized that our actions, in spite of God's grace and a degree of free will, are to some extent caused, the Roman Catholic account emphasizes human freedom. The church has stressed that human beings are free to choose good and reject evil or to choose evil and reject good. In the Catholic account, though God's grace can significantly influence the choice that humans make, we are also free to reject God's grace. But a scientific psychology would seem to qualify Roman Catholicism's emphasis on our capacity to make free choices. Psychology reveals the extent to which our freedom is restricted by our biology, our past and our present. And a scientific psychology suggests that psychological damage reduces even further our capacity to choose; the greater the damage done to our personality, the less we are able to make free choices. But psychology does not absolve us from striving with what little freedom we have, and with the help of God's grace, to avoid evil and to do good. And psychologists assert that the psychologically more whole (or holier) that we are, the more free we are to make moral choices. Psychologists, of course, stress that we should use what freedom we have to avoid wrongdoing and to choose what is right. But Simone Weil's notion of 'gravity' is a recognition of the power that natural forces, emphasized by psychology, have to limit human freedom.

Simone sees humans as existing within the two domains of grace and of gravity. She acknowledges the reality and power of the domain of gravity, of the relentless laws of cause and effect that impinge on our personality and cause our behaviour. But she also recognizes the domain of grace relating to a movement of divine love which liberates us and enables us to choose, to defy gravity and to grow upwards to God. However, Simone does not see God as present in grace and absent in gravity; she does not oppose the supernatural and natural. But, for Simone, the purpose and meaning that we seek in our lives are to be found only in the realm of grace, where divine love and goodness move the individual soul to God.

Simone Weil holds that the freedom which enables human

personality to defy gravity is a response to something beyond the material world. She sees human freedom in terms of a longing within personality for an absolute good outside space and time; she identifies this good with God. Whether or not this good is recognized by us for what it really is, Simone maintains that only our longing for this good beyond the world of space and time can raise us above matter and gravity. But Simone is never in doubt about the immense pressure exerted on human beings by gravity – by natural forces such as biology, past psychological experience and present social circumstances.

And the power over us of such natural forces is augmented by a more existential dimension to our lives. Modern existentialism affirms the existence of free human choice; but existential psychology also recognizes the extent to which our lives are fettered by a permeating despair, anxiety and sense of meaninglessness. Existential psychology emphasizes our awareness that we, and those we love, exist close to death and to the non-being from which we emerged. Such experiences are existential in the sense that they are simply part of being human, have nothing to do with past or present experience, and are inevitable. Existentialism sees that anxiety, despair, meaninglessness, and an awareness of the closeness of ourselves and those we love to nothingness, give to human life a crippling, driven quality.

Such existential elements are to be found in the thought of Thérèse of Lisieux. She has a sense of the seeming irrelevance of human life, and she recognizes an undertug of despair in her own and other people's lives. She refers several times in *Story of a Soul* to her own 'nothingness'. But Thérèse sees human nothingness in terms of an abyss of self face-to-face with the abyss of an infinite God of love and compassion. And one reason why this God regards us with such love and mercy, says Thérèse, is because 'He is perfectly aware of our fragile nature'.[3]

Catherine of Siena's *Dialogue* also displays elements of existential thought, with God referring to sin as non-being, as nothingness, as the opposite of being. And in the *Dialogue*, Catherine is told never to criticize others, since human judgment is based on externals. 'You must never pass judgment in human terms on anything you see or hear from anyone at all,'[4] God instructs her. The *Dialogue* stresses that only God knows what is happening within any human being. God says to Catherine: 'For often such a person's intention is good; there is no one who can judge the hidden heart.'[5] And God speaks to Catherine of a 'perverse law'[6] within her, causing her to rebel against God.

Julian of Norwich, too, is aware of the pressures on human beings. 'But because of the contradictions in us,' she says in the *Revelations of Divine Love*, 'we often fall into sin.'[7] God appears to suggest to her that sin cannot be avoided since it is inherent in being human; Jesus tells her that sin 'had to be'.[8] Julian seems to understand that God has some responsibility for sin. A Christian psychology would suggest that God is involved in each of us being what we are, biologically and psychologically, and in each of us being in our particular social situation. Julian seems to see sin existentially as some terrible wound, or a condition within ourselves and the world which leaves us damaged. The cure for this sin-sickness is to be found in God's love.

And since she has been told that sin cannot be avoided, Julian declares that we should not regard ourselves and others harshly but with compassion. Like many psychologists, Julian holds that people often blame themselves too much. 'But do not be too downcast,' she says, 'by the sin that overcomes you against your will. And here I understood that our Lord looks upon his servant with pity, not with blame.'[9] And she says that when we do sin, God unconditionally forgives us.

Julian sees that the harsh way in which often we regard others, and others judge us, contrasts with God's merciful perspective. Julian says of God: 'I saw him assign no whit of blame to us.'[10] She is particularly puzzled by the contrast between a judging Catholic Church and a loving God who does not blame us. Only God, says Julian, sees completely all that is occurring within us; and God, aware of our limitations and the pressures we are under, refuses to judge. Her explanation for a judging church and for God's refusal even to pass judgment might, in modern terms, be that God is a good psychologist, whereas the church of her time seemed to know little of human psychology.

Psychology stresses the extent to which human behaviour is, partly or largely, caused. Julian reports a certain inevitability to sin – 'it had to be'.[11] Psychology specifically draws attention to the pressures exerted on human beings, often unconsciously, by biology, past psychological experience and present social circumstances. Similarly, Simone's notion of 'gravity' suggests our actions are powerfully shaped by natural forces; Catherine's 'perverse law' possibly implies something similar. Existential psychology recognizes the despair and sense of our nothingness, referred to by Thérèse, which often constrain our lives. The findings of psychology incline us to a more tolerant and less judgmental view of others – and ourselves. And in the accounts of the four women, God emerges as a psychologist more likely than any human psychologist to observe the drunk in the gutter and ourselves – in Julian's words – 'with pity, not with blame'.[12]

3

The Psychology of Two Catholic Personalities

You should realize that wanting to make God's servants all walk in our own way – which could never be done, anyway – would be no different from setting down laws and rules for the Holy Spirit.

(Catherine of Siena, *Letter to Catherine di Scetto*)

You cannot fit the virtues into a legal structure without reducing them to dispositions to follow the rules. You can, however, fit law and obedience to law into a comfortable, though minor, niche in the project of growing up in the rich and variegated life of virtue.

(Herbert McCabe, Manuals and rule books, in *Understanding* Veritatis Splendor)

Would you know your Lord's meaning in this? Learn it well. Love was his meaning.

(Julian of Norwich, *Revelations of Divine Love*)

We are sometimes troubled to find that other people reject views that seem to us so obviously true; we may even find this threatening. The institutional Catholic Church seems frequently to have felt threatened by beliefs different from its own. The church persecuted and condemned Galileo partly because the pope and cardinals in Rome felt threatened by Galileo's view that the earth moved round the sun. With the sun and not the earth in the middle, the church's assertion that humans were the centre of God's creation seemed to be called in question; and the movement of the earth appeared to cast doubt on passages in scripture. Galileo's condemnation by pope and cardinals was a reaction of closed-minded personalities. Research demonstrates that closed-minded personalities have difficulty in accepting new ideas. But the research of Rokeach and others suggests, particularly, that closed minds feel threatened by views different from their own and that closed minds are prejudiced against people who hold views different from their own.

In the Middle Ages, a religious tradition holding beliefs different from those of Christianity existed within Catholic Europe. This was Judaism; and the Catholic Church brutally persecuted Jews. Among the several causes of this relentless persecution was that the institutional church felt threatened, psychologically, by the proximity of beliefs different from the church's own beliefs. Part of the institutional church's antisemitism might more accurately be termed anti-Judaism; the church was hostile to the Jewish faith and persecuted Jews who held to their own religious beliefs. The choice that Jews were sometimes offered, between death and conversion to Christianity, is evidence that the church's antisemitism was caused, in part, by the institutional church finding threatening the presence of others with different religious beliefs. Over the centuries, until as recently as Pope Pius IX's *Syllabus of Errors* in 1864, the Catholic Church has usually attempted to have other religions banned and to have Catholicism as the only faith permitted. This is the closed-minded Catholic personality at work, frequently feeling menaced by beliefs unlike its own, reacting defensively and often with hostility.

Rokeach found that whether our minds were closed or open is not necessarily related to what is believed, whether in areas such as religion, politics or psychology. We can be Catholic, Methodist, Socialist, Conservative, Freudian, Jungian, with a closed or open mind. Whether our mind is closed or open is largely dependent on the way in which we believe, on the personal psychology which underpins our beliefs. Usually, it is not so much, according to Rokeach, the content of our beliefs that determines whether our mind is closed or open, but the *manner* in which we believe.

So closed- and open-minded personalities cannot always be distinguished by what they believe. At any given time, closed- and open-minded Catholics might subscribe to more or less the same beliefs. What distinguishes between Catholics with closed minds and those with open minds is the different ways in which they hold these beliefs. Personalities with closed minds, like the pope and cardinals faced with Galileo's new ideas, are less open to change. Rokeach's research also shows that closed minds are more resistant to self-questioning than open minds. Significantly, Roman Catholic hierarchies have traditionally disapproved of any form of religious questioning.

But what particularly distinguishes between closed and open minds, in Rokeach's account, is the contrasting way in which they react to beliefs unlike their own and to people who hold these different beliefs. The hostility of the medieval and Renaissance church to Judaism is symptomatic of the closed mind. In contrast, open minds emphasize how much their own beliefs have in common with those of others. Open-minded Catholics stress their common origins with Judaism; they do not feel menaced by the different beliefs of others; they see all religions as ultimately worshipping the same God; they emphasize the similarities that their own beliefs have with those of other Christian traditions, such as Anglicans and Methodists, and with other religions generally.

Closed minds stress and magnify differences between their own beliefs and those of others. Closed-minded Catholics emphasize what they regard as the uniqueness of the Christian God and stress differences between Roman Catholics and others. An extreme example of this emphasis on difference is the now discarded Catholic doctrine of 'No salvation outside the church'. A much more trivial example, but illustrative of the same preoccupation, is the hierarchy's past ban on Roman Catholics participating in non-Catholic ceremonies, such as the weddings of non-Catholic relatives. In the recent past, strictly speaking a Catholic wife and her children should not have said grace at mealtimes with a non-Catholic husband and father!

Closed-minded Catholics assert dogmatically that church teaching is definitive and final. But modern psychology suggests that frequently such dogmatism is not an expression of certainty but a symptom of doubt. In the late nineteenth century, senior members of the hierarchy declared that the then recent definition of papal infallibility gave to the church complete assurance of the truth. But psychology would suggest that such emphatic declarations are often indicative of uncertainty. The psychological reality is that dogmatism often masks the insecurity of closed-minded Catholics, who find disturbing the possibility of church authority being fallible. Psychological theory and research seem to suggest that closed-minded Catholics are usually troubled by doubt.

So why do closed-minded Catholics feel threatened by beliefs at variance with their own and why are they prejudiced against those who hold different beliefs? Why did a closed-minded church in the past feel so psychologically menaced by those who did not accept Catholicism, such as Jews, heretics and pagans, that the church persecuted them? One cause is in the uncertainty that closed-minded Catholics have about their own beliefs; the proximity of people with different beliefs aggravates and adds to their uncertainty. However, doubts do not of themselves cause us to be closed-minded and dogmatic.

The problem for closed minds is that they have doubts and cannot admit to their doubts. Catholics often become closed-minded when they are unsure about their religious faith but cannot acknowledge their uncertainty, even to themselves. Open-minded Catholics might also have doubts but can admit to them. Open-minded Catholics, aware of their own uncertainty, can admit – at least to themselves – that their own beliefs probably do not contain the whole truth; as a result, they can recognize truth in the beliefs of others. Depth psychology suggests that we are closed-minded and dogmatic when we are uncertain and have doubts, but our doubts and uncertainty remain unconscious.

The difference between Catholics with closed and open minds can be expressed in terms of whether their doubts and uncertainties are unconscious or conscious. The dogmatic closed minds of many Catholics express not certainty but doubt, and a doubt about their own beliefs so disturbing that they cannot acknowledge these doubts even to themselves. The closed minds of some Catholics protect them from their own uncertainty. When we cannot admit our uncertainty, we dislike and might even persecute others for not holding the beliefs of which we ourselves are unsure. With priests, bishops and popes the problem is increased by their official positions making it more difficult for them to acknowledge their own uncertainty, even to themselves. Popes and prelates, troubled by doubts and unable to admit them, have probably in the past sometimes persecuted others with different beliefs partly in an attempt to bolster their own faith.

Keats, the poet, writes of a 'negative capability' which he sees as a willingness to remain in uncertainties, doubts, mysteries. Such would seem to characterize the open-minded Catholic. This negative capability of Keats is not an abdication of intellectual activity, nor a fear of decision or commitment, but is usually the result of recognizing the full complexity of ideas, truths, principles, beliefs. Where a choice or a decision has to be made, the open-minded personality does so acknowledging the uncertainties involved. The negative capability of the open-minded Catholic personality sees the search for religious truth as involving uncertainty and a faith which, for most of us, never becomes certainty but always remains faith.

History would seem to suggest that great crimes against humanity are committed not by people who accept and live with their uncertainty, but by those who claim with absolute certainty that they are right. Violence has been done to others by popes, cardinals and bishops claiming dogmatically that the beliefs of Catholicism are absolute truth. But such dogmatism is, psychologically, often the product of unadmitted and unconscious doubt about Catholic belief. The institutional church's refusal to accept and live with uncertainty has been one cause of the church's persecution of others with different beliefs.

The closed mind seems related, psychologically, to authoritarianism. And research by Adorno and others, published as *The Authoritarian Personality*, adds further to our understanding of the causes of the institutional church's dogmatism, intolerance and persecution of others. The Adorno study, which began as a study of antisemitism, revealed a constellation of traits which tend to cluster together into what the researchers termed 'the authoritarian personality'.

Researchers demonstrated that people hostile to Jews are almost always hostile to others as well. People who are antisemitic dislike or hate a variety of groups. Since the groups that are the target of a particular person's hostility often differ considerably, the hostility cannot be related to the characteristics of these varying groups, but must originate within the prejudiced person. This is illustrated, in the Adorno research, by prejudiced people expressing antagonism towards fictitious groups with names made up by the researchers – and which did not exist! So the bigotry of prejudiced people must originate from within themselves, since their prejudice is unrelated to features of the particular groups towards whom they feel antagonism. The researchers concluded that prejudice is the product of a certain type of personal psychology. *The Authoritarian Personality* study revealed that the hostility of prejudiced people is really directed at any social group that they see as unlike themselves. Prejudiced people share with closed-minded personalities dislike or hatred for those whom they regard as significantly different from themselves.

Adorno and his fellow researchers arrived at further characterizations of the prejudiced person. What especially typified this personality was an obsession with authority and power – hence the researchers' term 'authoritarian personality'. The Adorno study demonstrated that prejudice and intolerance are directly related to authoritarianism. The research also found that authoritarian personalities tend to have very conservative views; they tend to be rigidly attached to conventional values and to 'things as they are'. Authoritarian personalities, with their attachment to 'things as they are', condemn and would punish people who reject their own conventional values. And, in a manner reminiscent of the institutional Roman Catholic Church, authoritarian personalities also display an excessive interest in the supposed sexual goings-on of others, believing that other people are constantly indulging in wild sexual activities. At the same time, authoritarian personalities regard their own group, which they idealize, as pure and blameless. Significantly, papal statements have often contrasted the supposedly evil goings-on of the secular world with an idealized account of the Catholic Church.

There might be several different ways in which an individual becomes authoritarian. I have previously suggested how the pressures of society partly mould our personality and form our views; and the personalities, values and prejudices of Catholics have often been shaped by a Catholic authoritarian tradition. But Adorno and his researchers explore one particular cause of the authoritarian personality, namely, childhood experience. Influenced by psycho-analytic ideas, they argue that authoritarian personalities, with their hostility towards people unlike themselves, are the product of a certain type of childhood. And *The Authoritarian Personality* study regards the way in which parents handle their children's anger as crucial.

A certain amount of anger is inevitable in our early years because of the frustrations of childhood and because parental discipline further frustrates us; such frustration causes anger. But child-rearing involves parents having to direct and shape children's behaviour, and what *The Authoritarian Personality* notes is that parents who are unsure of themselves correct and criticize their children particularly harshly. The result is that children of insecure parents are likely to be particularly angry and aggressive.

More importantly, insecure parents cannot handle their children's anger. When someone has made us angry, the obvious target for our anger and aggression is that person. But the children of insecure parents cannot express their anger and aggression against their parents, because these particularly punitive and in-secure parents will not allow them to do so. Eventually it is not only fear that prevents these children expressing anger against their parents. Since they have never been allowed to criticize their insecure parents, or have felt too frightened even to feel angry with them, these children end up seeing their parents in the way that the parents want to be seen, as ideal mothers and fathers. Idealizing the in-group to which one belongs, and those with authority in the in-group, characterizes the authoritarian personality.

In close human relationships there is usually an element of ambivalence; we like our friends but at times they irritate and annoy us; we love our husbands or wives or partners but often feel hostile towards them – and they do towards us! We have to learn to cope with liking and disliking the same person, and the ambivalence involves a tension which is painful. When children have parents confident enough to be able to take their anger, they learn to tolerate ambivalence and to live with the tension. But children of parents who are unsure of themselves never learn to handle the ambivalence of close relationships. As a result, they split what they feel into love and anger. They project their loving feelings on to their parents, idealizing them; as adults, they will say their mother was a saint. And they divert their anger elsewhere; as adults, their anger and aggression are directed against vulnerable minority groups that they see as significantly different from themselves.

The Adorno research reports that children who felt helpless in front of their intimidating parents grow into adults who feel powerless before authority. But, as adults, they try to make themselves feel powerful by identifying with a strong authority which they idealize, and by despising the weak. Authoritarian personalities angry as adults, as once they were as children, give themselves a false sense of power by lording it over those helpless beneath them. Adorno's research describes the relations of authoritarian personalities with other people as like riding a bicycle – bending over the handle-bars, then kicking the pedals. The authoritarian personality bows submissively before authority figures, then kicks subordinates below. The Nazi, abject before the Führer, directs his aggression away from terrifying authority towards powerless minorities, and doing so he takes to himself the power of being a mini-Führer. The aggression of Catholic authoritarians is partly rooted in a similar ambivalence; they divert unconscious hostility, emerging from submission before an authoritarian church, on to minority groups that they regard as different from themselves.

Whether a Catholic becomes authoritarian because of childhood experience of threatening parents, or through conformity to an authoritarian tradition, the Catholic authoritarian personality sees life as controlled – at a conscious level approves of life being controlled – by an external authority, such as the pope or Job's type of God. Before the power of popes and the institutional church, Catholic authoritarians regard themselves as abject and insignificant; but they feel powerful and significant by identifying with a powerful, idealized church – and by persecuting minority groups in the name of that church. History suggests that when the power of the papacy and the institutional church was at its most absolute Catholics were at their most hostile to Jews, heretics, gay people, non-Catholics, non-believers, supposed 'witches' and others whom they regarded as unlike themselves in some way.

The institutional church has been reluctant to acknowledge the reality and extent of Catholicism's history of antisemitism, lasting for nearly fifteen hundred years. The church's antisemitism might have its roots, historically, in hostility to the Jewish faith and to Jews remaining faithful to Judaism, but such hostility developed into a persecution of Jews as a community and a people. The church has been particularly unwilling to acknowledge the institutional church's own responsibility and guilt. But research, such as *The Authoritarian Personality*, suggests that Catholic antisemitism would partly have been a product of the authoritarian values and structure of the church. Authoritarian institutions, like authoritarian personalities, need a target for their aggression. The target should preferably be powerless since authoritarian institutions, like authoritarian personalities, are great respecters of power and prefer to persecute those not able to fight back. An authoritarian papacy and hierarchy, needing a vulnerable target for their hostility, have been largely responsible for Catholic antisemitism.

The modern papacy is attempting to rid the church of the antisemitism and bigotry of the past. But the papacy and the institutional church remain authoritarian, and *The Authoritarian Personality* study demonstrates that prejudice and intolerance are a product of authoritarianism. The Adorno studies would suggest that prejudice and intolerance will continue to characterize the institutional church while its values and structure remain authoritarian.

The Catholic liberal personality has always been aware of the dangers of an authoritarian church. In recent times, the Catholic liberal personality has been shaped by a liberal (humanistic) psychology influenced by existentialism, Jungian and other depth psychologies, the neo-Freudianism of Fromm and Fairbairn, and modern ideas about the self and self-actualization of Abraham Maslow and others. There is evidence from psychology that the individual is diminished by excessive submission to authority. Stanley Milgram's *Obedience to Authority* study showed that in obeying authority we tend to see ourselves just as agents of our superiors. Milgram's research revealed that, seeing ourselves as merely agents of authority, we regard ourselves as not wholly responsible for what we do in obedience to authority's orders.

Catherine of Siena's *Dialogue* is occasionally characterized by an excessive emphasis on obedience to the institutional church; to this extent, Catherine is authoritarian. But Catherine prefers to see such obedience as the response of love, not as mere conformity to authority; Catherine also values obedience because it dents human pride and self-will. And though Catherine was a great respecter of the institutional church, even at a time when the papacy was exceptionally corrupt, she holds that our decisions have to be our own decisions. What we think and do should be the result not of external constraints but of our love for God. She stressed that ordinary uneducated people often find the light of God's truth within themselves, even when their religious superiors – in spite of their learning – fall short. A Catholic liberal psychology holds that in excessive obedience to the church we are likely to abdicate personal responsibility and become less able to behave in a moral way, and our capacity to do good diminishes.

In contrast, for the authoritarian Catholic, the way to follow conscience is simply by obeying the church. As late as the nineteenth century, popes were describing liberty of conscience as an absurd and ludicrous maxim; and Thérèse's life at the close of the nineteenth century is usually stressed as that of a dutiful daughter of the church. The reality is that Thérèse was not excessively preoccupied with submission to authority. Her autobiography, *Story of a Soul*, reads as the record of a woman who made relationships central to her life and who struggled to achieve personal independence, relying on her experience of God and Christ to do both. Thérèse saw herself as ordinary, and her belief that God is particularly inclined to love ordinary people gave her the confidence for a direct relationship with God. In her autobiography, we observe Thérèse relying less on obedience to authority and more on what Newman called the 'first vicar of Christ', namely, conscience.

Influenced by existentialism, a liberal psychology regards conscience as the voice of the existential self. Similarly, the Catholic liberal personality sees personal conscience as the voice of our self calling us to be true to the image of God within us. A Catholic liberal psychology, while recognizing the importance of the church in shaping our experience, holds that spiritual and moral growth involves moving from extreme dependence on the external authority of the church to greater reliance on our own internal experience. Thérèse saw herself as an obedient Catholic and she was helped by the church to a relationship with Christ; but Thérèse emerges in her life and thought with an unmistakable personal identity, and she moves to a direct relationship with God which goes far beyond 'being a Catholic'. Catholic liberal psychology maintains that spiritual and psychological growth requires that our own personal experience becomes central in separating wrong from right, bad from good. Here too our conscience can partly be relied on; God tells Catherine in the *Dialogue* that 'the soul by its very nature always craves what is good'.[1]

Authoritarian personalities can rightly counter that personal conscience and our inner experience may be in error. And God warns Catherine: 'Still it is true that the soul, if blinded by selfishness, cannot recognize or discern what is truly good and profitable for soul and body.'[2] An authoritarian Catholic regards conforming to church rules, and believing all that the church teaches, as the best defence against such dangers. For the Catholic authoritarian personality, faith in general, belief in certain dogmas, subscribing to certain rules and discipleship of Christ are not a product of personal experience or of a thought-out position, but result from submission to authority. Catholic authoritarian personalities believe in an external God whose will is made known to them through popes, cardinals and bishops.

The Catholic authoritarian personality tends to regard the existence of God as a fact that can be taken for granted, confirmed by church teaching. The First Vatican Council condemned the view that belief in God's existence cannot be attained by reason. Regardless of whether God can be discovered by reason alone, a Catholic liberal psychology sees any such God as at best a God of the philosophers, much as in modern times a God believed in solely on the authority of the church is almost irrelevant. For the Catholic liberal personality, only the God discovered also in personal experience is relevant, since only this God affects our lives. Authoritarian Catholics tend to take the teaching of the church as a substitute for their own personal experience, using church authority as a bulwark against religious doubt. A Catholic liberal psychology recognizes the necessity of acknowledging doubt. The Catholic liberal personality attempts to discover by a combination of experience, feeling, faith and reason, heart as well as head, a divine presence within, Julian's God 'nearer to us than our own soul'[3] and 'the ground on which our soul stands'.[4] A Catholic liberal psychology maintains that belief in God's existence may, partly, be a product of membership of a religious tradition but needs also to be a personal decision.

Karl Rahner, a twentieth-century Roman Catholic theologian, sees contemporary Catholicism in a process of moving from a past situation where church membership has been sustained by a Christian culture. Catholic authoritarian personalities still tend to see their own worth largely in terms of being members of the church and acknowledged as such by others. The authoritarian personality's sense of his or her own value emerges not from within but is bestowed from outside, from being recognized as a good Catholic by the church. But Rahner maintains that in the future the church will consist of those endeavouring to achieve, in a secular society, a personal decision and commitment of faith.

In contrast with a Catholic liberal psychology which holds that we can love others only if we love ourselves, Catholic authoritarian personalities regard valuing ourselves as dangerous self-love; they tend to see themselves as bad in God's sight and, to alleviate their guilt, typically seek out religious authority to whom they can confess. The practice of confession, with the priest alone having the power to forgive sins, further illustrates this dependence on the church. A liberal psychology sees the dependency of the confessional, unless handled with psychological sensitivity and expertise, as likely to retard an individual's personal and moral growth. More generally, a liberal psychology holds that an excessively top/down church, reactivating childhood fears of cutting safe bonds with parents, obstructs psychological development.

Jung comments that more important than confessing our 'sins' is discovering why there is so much in us that needs to be forgiven.

And research indicates that authoritarian personalities feel inadequate and have low opinions of themselves. The Adorno study might suggest that authoritarian personalities, particularly, feel a need to be forgiven for the aggression that is within them as a result of their childhood experience. An existential account sees, as adding to this anger from childhood, resentment generated in adult life by a denial of appropriate freedom. Existential psychology would suggest that Catholics often feel a need to be forgiven for the animosity within them, caused by excessive submission to an authoritarian church, and for their hostility to others emerging from such animosity. A Catholic liberal psychology values love above submission and obedience. To this end, the Catholic liberal personality stresses the importance of knowing that we are loved unconditionally by God; Thérèse of Lisieux refers in her autobiography to 'the burning Abyss of this Love'.[5]

The Catholic liberal personality accepts the traditional Christian view that moral development requires the effort of free will: we grow away from evil and develop in goodness partly by living unselfishly, by exercising self-control to check our dangerous desires, by using our will to act for the benefit of others. But a Catholic liberal psychology, while regarding such effort as necessary and involving self-sacrifice, declares that something more is needed for us to grow in goodness. A liberal psychology maintains that much of the wrong that we do is partly a consequence of our lives being unlived and unfulfilled. We harm others and fail to love them because we are crippled psychologically and unhappy. If we move to greater wholeness in our lives and become more fulfilled, then the bad in us diminishes and the good increases. We might be unhappy because we do wrong to others but, according to a Catholic liberal psychology, we also do wrong to others because we are unhappy.

Existentialism recognizes anxiety, despair, meaninglessness and a sense of void as characterizing human life; Thérèse records in *Story of a Soul* how she suffered from these experiences. The authoritarian personality, according to existential psychology, uses religion as a defence against such experiences; religious belief becomes a bulwark protecting us from this disturbing existential dimension in our lives. The Catholic liberal personality accepts, as Thérèse did, that there is no defence against these experiences; they have to be acknowledged, felt and eventually accepted. The Catholic liberal personality sees that the answer to life's existential elements is found, not in submission to the church but, as Thérèse's autobiography reports, in abandonment to God.

Catholic liberal personalities, aware of the risks in both a liberal and authoritarian strategy, opt for the liberal strategy because of its basis in love; they see Christ in the New Testament establishing love, rather than rules and law, as the definitive basis for human living. A Catholic liberal psychology does not deny the place of duty, obligation and law in morality and recognizes the qualified value of obedience to rules. But the liberal personality sees where, in the history of church and state, unmitigated application of rules and law leads; in England, at the beginning of the nineteenth century, people could be hanged for petty theft.

A liberal psychology's emphasis on love reduces the stress on rules which is central to Catholic authoritarianism. The Catholic liberal personality does not regard rules as irrelevant; there are valid rules about marriage, such as that one should be faithful to one's partner. But, according to a Catholic liberal psychology, Christ came to replace a legalistic morality, and the truly Christian reason for being faithful in marriage is love of one's wife or husband. Similarly, the Catholic liberal personality, while recognizing adultery as wrong, does not inevitably pass judgment and condemn the married man or woman who is unfaithful. The action is judged but not the person; Catholic liberal psychology sees Christ condemning sin but not condemning the sinner. God instructs Catherine, in the *Dialogue*, not to judge others; God specifically points out that no human being ever knows enough about another to be in a position to pass judgment. Psychology recognizes the extent to which our freedom is constrained by our body, past experience and present situation. A liberal psychology holds that people are more likely to grow in goodness if, rather than being judged, they are understood and accepted.

In contrast, the Catholic authoritarian personality not only values judging and condemning as important but tends to emphasize the judgment and condemnation of individual acts. The liberal personality, even when a person's individual act seems wrong, regards such an action as needing to be evaluated in terms of a person's overall orientation. A married person's adultery might best be understood in terms of the search for a loving relationship, missing in her present marriage, where she and her husband find themselves disastrously incompatible. A Catholic liberal psychology sees individual acts mattering less than a person's basic overall orientation; significantly, Christ's Beatitudes relate to overall dispositions. The Catholic liberal personality emphasizes understanding and, particularly, understanding the whole person and the person's general attitude or disposition. A woman or man is more likely to forgive a husband or wife's present moodiness, or infidelity, in the context of the partner's love over the years; the Catholic liberal personality sees God as doing the same, but more so.

Catholic liberal psychology holds Christ's revelation as less to do with obedience to rules and more about growing in relationships of love with God and other human beings; such a perspective sees morality largely in terms of whatever makes us develop psychologically, brings us closer to God and makes us more Christ-like. Doing wrong cripples human beings psychologically and prevents them from approaching closer to God and others. For Catherine and Catherine's God, the tragedy of sin is partly that it damages and destroys the beauty of human beings. In the *Dialogue*, God shows Catherine the beauty that all human beings have, simply by virtue of being human. And a Catholic liberal psychology stresses the dignity and value of every human person before God.

God tells Catherine in the *Dialogue* 'I am supreme eternal Truth',[6] and the Catholic authoritarian personality holds the 'supreme eternal truth' of Catherine's God to be perfectly revealed in the teachings of the church. Catholic liberal personalities, while acknowledging that the church's claims impose obligations, attempt to reconcile contemporary teaching of the church with their own inner truth. A Catholic liberal psychology holds that in the area of religion we are confronted by truths that go beyond the grasp of intellect and cannot be contained in clear-cut definitions. Such religious truths become meaningful only in the free discovery and experience of the individual. Both Catherine and Thérèse emphasize differences between people, maintaining that there are different ways and paths to God.

A Catholic liberal psychology sees faith as of most value when the product of personal thought and feeling; in an individual's life, belief and faith may partly originate from church membership, but such faith has eventually to develop into intellectual and emotional conviction. Even if the individual lives within a community of believers, for the Catholic liberal personality faith should be rooted in personal experience and needs to become personal conviction. Thérèse, in her autobiography and letters, emerges not as the conforming nun of some of her biographers but as a woman eventually able in her life to rely on her own experience of God – even when that God seems distant. She emerges as someone not continuously referring to the rules of the church but who trusts her own judgment and self-knowledge.

Thérèse anticipates modern psychology in stressing the value of our own experience and in seeing that we are not truly adult until we can rely on our experience. Thérèse recognizes the importance of the rules that are part of our circumstances; in her own situation, these were the rules of the Carmelite Order and of the church. But she holds that our own understanding and insights are to be respected. Thérèse seems to be saying that our self can only really relate to God and others when we go beyond the level of a self that merely follows rules. A liberal psychology, similarly, contends that we only have a self which can relate to and love others when our self is more than just the product of conformity to rules. Indeed, a liberal psychology contends that only if we go beyond rules do we really have a self! And without a real self we degenerate into the authoritarian personality's anger and resentment, which existentialism recognizes as a protest against the feeling of not really existing.

In Thérèse's life and writings, psychological and spiritual development is about relationships with God and others, characterized not by domination and control but by personal independence, equality and an increased sense of self-worth. She rejects a guilt-ridden, fearful and rule-obsessed Catholicism and proposes instead a faith where God is characterized by mercy, love, compassion.

A liberal Catholic psychology maintains that obedience to the institutional church cannot relieve us of responsibility for what we do, nor become a substitute for personal beliefs, nor take the place of our own experience. Loving God and others cannot be done for me by anyone else, not even by a sacramental church. As a child I believed in the existence of God because I accepted what my parents taught me; but this belief needs to become a matter of my personal conviction, ideally based on some level of experiencing God. A Catholic liberal psychology holds that only religious truths that are lived and experienced have the power to move and change us.

The Catholic liberal personality sees love as central to our lives and to Christ's teaching; in the *Dialogue* God tells Catherine, 'All I want is love.'[7] The authoritarian Catholic, recognizing that people cannot be made to love God and their neighbour, values particularly obedience to the church, to be achieved, if necessary, through coercion – in the past often by violence, in the present by psychological pressures such as fear. In contrast, a Catholic liberal psychology holds that freedom from coercion is essential for human beings to grow in love of God and neighbour. The liberal personality sees that a controlling and authoritarian Catholic Church forms personalities equipped to obey and fear but unable to do the one necessary thing – love; love requires freedom. Julian of Norwich disapproves of fear in our relationship with God, contrasting fear not with courage but with love. For Thérèse, too, the relevant motivation for the Christian is not fear and submission but love – '*the law of Love* has succeeded to the law of fear'.[8] In the closed-minded authoritarian personality and the open-minded liberal personality we have two extremes; and most individual Catholics are somewhere to be found on a continuum between the two. But modern psychology sees psychological growth partly in terms of a shift and development, from a closed-minded and obedience-obsessed authoritarian personality to an open-minded and liberal personality characterized above all by love.

Julian of Norwich contrasted a loving God with a Catholic Church seemingly emphasizing judgment. If the Catholic Church of Julian's time was harsh, judgmental and persecuting, though its God is loving, this would be partly because the institutional church of her time was controlled by popes, cardinals and bishops with closed-minded and authoritarian personalities. In contrast, God's personality seemed – and seems – open-minded and liberal!

But the institutional church of Julian's time was harsh, judgmental and persecuting, when God is so loving, not only because of the personalities of popes, cardinals and bishops. Human actions are only in part products of our individual personalities; all of us are powerfully shaped by the values and structures of the social organizations to which we belong. The authoritarianism of many Catholics is also the product of the values and structure of an institutional church within an authoritarian tradition.

The defining characteristic of both the liberal personality and the liberal tradition is love. Julian, reflecting for many years on God's revelations to her, eventually decides their significance: 'Love was his meaning. Who showed it you? Love. What did he show you? Love. Why did he show you? For love. Hold fast to this and you shall learn and know more about love, but you shall never know nor learn about anything except love for ever.'[9]

4

The Psychology of Two Catholic Traditions

But she is guilty of an abuse of power when she claims to force love and intelligence to model their language upon her own. This abuse of power is not of God.
(Simone Weil on the Catholic Church, *Waiting on God*)

Christians believe that anyone who is faithful to the dictates of his or her conscience is following this intimate movement in God towards God.
(Karl Rahner and Karl-Heinz Weger, *Our Christian Faith*)

In a higher world it is otherwise, but here below to live is to change, and to be perfect is to have changed often.
(John Henry Newman, *Essay on the Development of Christian Doctrine*)

I was dismayed to learn, as a schoolboy, that throughout the nineteenth century popes had condemned democracy. My Jesuit teacher's explanation, that 'God is not a democratic concept', seemed unsatisfactory. Papal condemnation of democracy and of liberal values related to democracy, such as equality, human rights, freedom of conscience, freedom of religious belief, was the product of a Catholic authoritarian tradition.

From the beginning to almost the close of the nineteenth century, popes condemned social movements which wished to replace absolute monarchs and unrepresentative governments with democratic forms of government. Throughout most of the nineteenth century, popes seemed indifferent to reforms that would improve the condition of ordinary men and women. As a consequence, many working people in Europe left the church and turned to trade unions and political movements for help in improving their lives. Papal indifference to social reform was not to stop with the end of the nineteenth century. At the beginning of the twentieth, Pope Pius X declared the inequalities of class and social position in human society to be divinely ordained. But Pius X especially affirmed the rightness of hierarchy, inequality, authority and obedience within the church, emphasizing particularly his own authority as pope. Simone Weil saw the church's preoccupation with its own authority expressed in two words, *anathema sit* – Let him be accursed. These words, used in the past by an authoritarian church for centuries to denounce and excommunicate, usually led to prison, torture, death. Simone claimed the two words were partly what stopped her becoming a Catholic.

The central place of equality as a value in the twentieth century has forced the church to abandon its view that inequalities in secular society are divinely ordained and inevitable. The institutional church has done so with reluctance; a more equal society creates pressure for a less hierarchical structure in the church. But though the authoritarian tradition has dominated the Roman Catholic Church for much of its history, there also exists within the church a liberal tradition which seems more in the spirit of the Gospels.

Social psychology research demonstrates that authoritarian organizations have characteristic values and structures. Authoritarian institutions regard their own authority and power as primary; their structure is hierarchical, and the institution's interests are regarded as prior to those of the individual. In an authoritarian organization, personal conscience is subordinated to authority. In the authoritarian tradition, fear is regarded as a legitimate means of enforcing obedience; a religious authoritarianism not only wishes to subordinate to its authority people's behaviour but also what they think and feel.

Social psychological research, such as Milgram's *Obedience to Authority* study, demonstrates the dangers in obedience. Milgram's research reveals a three-step process typical in situations of obedience.

First, I join the organization and, by doing so, make a degree of commitment to an authority. I join a political party; I am born into the church or I convert to Catholicism; I become a priest or nun. When I enter any hierarchically structured organization, particularly where obedience to authority is emphasized, I tend to stop regarding myself as an independent person personally responsible for what I do; I begin seeing myself as an agent of the organization, subject to the institution and responsible to its authority. Once I see myself as merely an agent of the organization I regard it as right that I should be directed by others senior to me and obey their orders.

There are a variety of experiences which have predisposed me to react in this way. I learnt as a child to do as my parents told me; instructions, like 'keep away from the hot oven', proved to be for my own good; and my parents also punished me if I disobeyed. Similarly, as an adult I find it is wise to abide by society's rules, such as driving on the left (or right) side of the road. Like my parents, society rewards me for obeying its rules; the role of dissident is always difficult. As an adult, there is usually an additional reason for obeying authority in an organization to which I belong – I usually accept its overall objectives. I am predisposed to accepting party or church rules because I originally joined the political party, or became a priest of the church, because I agreed with its objectives.

No longer regarding myself as an independent person responsible for my actions, but as an agent of the institution, I begin to see things differently; this is step two. Where I might once have wondered if I was inflicting unnecessary pain on children, I now see myself as an obedient nun, conscientiously chastizing young sinners on Mother Superior's orders, to save them from hell fire. Milgram's research would suggest that, as a consequence of this second step, medieval inquisitors probably did not see themselves as barbarous torturers of fellow human beings but as dutiful agents of the institutional church, ridding the church of heresy. People at this second stage, regarding themselves as agents of those in authority over them, come to adopt authority's definition of the situation.

Milgram observes that at this second stage morality can take on a perverse and terrifying twist. The inquisitor no longer sees right or wrong in terms of what he does, such as 'I am burning a living human being at the stake'; he now sees right and wrong in terms of how well he is obeying his superior's order to rid the church of heretics. The medieval or Renaissance bishop, persecuting heretics and Jews, does not regard himself as disobedient to Christ's command of love; he sees himself as obedient to a pope preaching that heretics are evil and that Jews murdered God, and that both threaten the church. According to Milgram, right and wrong are now perceived in terms of how well or badly authority's instructions are obeyed. But as a result, I have now abdicated personal moral responsibility, regarding myself solely as an agent of the organization, accepting authority's account of what I am doing – 'I am eliminating the cancer of heresy from God's church', 'I am punishing the killers of God', 'I am forcibly converting heretics for their own eternal good'. At this stage, morality is perversely seen in terms of how well or badly I implement the orders of authority.

The third and final step occurs when the individual becomes psychologically locked into the situation. People become locked into authority situations and, according to Milgram, often do terrible things because they have difficulty disobeying in the situation. From childhood onwards so much has predisposed us to obedience that disobeying authority is difficult. I might not agree with what is happening, but I cannot betray the party or criticize the pope's latest pronouncement. It is particularly difficult for the individual to show dissent in an authoritarian tradition with its emphasis on obedience. For a bishop to bring the church into disrepute by exposing abuse or sleaze behind closed Catholic doors is, in the authoritarian tradition, particularly to be condemned. Milgram's research, demonstrating the effects of obedience, explains why the workings of individual conscience and personal responsibility diminish significantly within an authoritarian and hierarchical organization.

According to social psychology, what really matters for the organization in an authoritarian tradition is its own survival; authority exercises power to do whatever is necessary for the institution to survive and prosper, even if individuals have to be sacrificed. And when the institution seems threatened, the authoritarian tradition holds that the search for truth, too, must be subordinated. When in 1859 the *Origin of Species* was published, Darwin joined Copernicus, Galileo, Descartes, Pascal, Locke, Voltaire, Rousseau, Kant, John Stuart Mill and other originators of modern thought on the papacy's *Index of Books Forbidden to Catholics*. In the nineteenth century, the institutional church's attempt to stifle new thought within Catholicism caused many European intellectuals, especially scientists, to abandon the church and Catholicism to lose touch with modernity.

Within an authoritarian institution, according to social psychology, authority simply assumes its legitimacy and rarely attempts to justify its decisions and orders. Papal encyclicals are characterized by assertions and are often short on argument and evidence. 'Bishops,' one nineteenth-century Roman Catholic bishop is reputed to have said, 'do not argue; they condemn.' Social psychology points out that where power is prized, no one in authority feels a need to provide reasons. Pope Paul VI established a commission to examine the question of artifical methods of birth control within marriage. The commission concluded, partly from evidence and reason, that decisions on birth control should be left to the conscience of the couple. This was not the Pope's view, and he rejected the committee's conclusions. The result, in 1968, was *Humanae Vitae*, a short encyclical, thin on argument, with the minimum of evidence, forbidding Catholics artificial methods of birth control. The encyclical is characteristic of the authoritarian tradition, which holds that ultimately matters are not decided by reason and evidence but by the exercise of authority.

Social psychology recognizes that in an authoritarian tradition power is typically located in a visible external authority. In the Catholic authoritarian tradition, God's authority is now specifically seen as located in the pope and the Roman Curia. After the definition of papal infallibility in the nineteenth century, bishops frequently addressed the pope as 'sole fountain of truth'. In the authoritarian tradition, the church is divided into the *teaching church* of pope, cardinals and bishops, which governs and rules, and the *learning church* of the laity, which listens and obeys. Popes and bishops in the authoritarian tradition regard individual Catholics as unable to decide right and wrong for themselves; this has to be decided for them by the authority of the institutional church. The parallel is with parents reluctant to allow their children to grow up, seeing danger in sons and daughters, no longer completely subordinate, doing what they themselves think is right.

In contrast, a Catholic liberal tradition, holding to the centrality of love, sees danger in an exaggerated emphasis on obedience, especially to an authority not accountable to anyone and subject to no control. Catholic liberal tradition recognizes that conscience, and our views on right and wrong, are shaped in interaction with other people and by our life in the church. But the liberal tradition, like parents aware that children eventually have to find their own way, holds that each of us must eventually discover values and beliefs to live by for ourself. The Catholic liberal tradition, though emphasizing the importance of church membership in shaping our path to God, recognizes also that the way to God for each of us is partly a product of our unique biologies, histories and circumstances. In the *Dialogue*, God stresses to Catherine that all must find their own way to God and that there are a variety of paths. Thérèse, too, conscious of rich spiritual lives among ordinary people, believed that human beings, guided by God, have little need for constant supervision by the church.

In contrast, the Catholic authoritarian tradition returns time and again to obedience, even regarding sin in terms of disobedience to authority. In the authoritarian tradition, if a man commits adultery his sin consists largely in disobeying the rules of God and the church; betrayal and hurt done to his wife take second place. The God of the authoritarian church is the God of Job, whom we obey because *He* is more powerful than us. This God does not give Adam and Eve reasons why they should not eat from the forbidden tree; the tree is not in someone else's garden! The prohibition on the tree makes clear that God is in charge; in the authoritarian tradition, the sin that Adam and Eve are guilty of in eating the fruit is disobedience. The authoritarian church stresses guilt, but not a guilt related to regret at offending someone we love, as the unfaithful husband might feel. In an authoritarian tradition, sin and guilt are to do with fear, particularly fear of offending a God who would punish us for our disobedience.

Catherine's God emphasizes that in religious life all must obey their superiors. God's obsession in the *Dialogue* with the authority of religious superiors seems best understood, in the context of the dissolute lives of clergy in Catherine's time, as partly her projection.

But Catherine's God especially wants such obedience to be motivated by love rather than fear. And Catherine moves particularly to a more liberal tradition when, in the *Dialogue*, God stresses personal relationship: 'I am infinite Good and I therefore require of you infinite desire.'[1] Thérèse, too, mindful of Christ's love for each of us, firmly locates herself in the Catholic liberal tradition when she asserts the dignity of every individual, uniquely loved by God.

Many explanations have been suggested for the church's authoritarian tradition. Liberal Catholic historians have regretted that, under the Emperor Constantine, Christianity in the fourth century became, effectively, the religion of the Roman empire. 'The church,' says Simone Weil in *Gateway to God*, 'has borne too many evil fruits for there not to have been some mistake made at the beginning.'[2] According to historians, through the next hundred or so years, as Christianity became the religion of an authoritarian Roman empire, the church moved from being a persecuted church to becoming a church which persecuted heretics, pagans and Jews. Historians record that antisemitism continued within the institutional church through the centuries that followed. But a significantly more authoritarian church, far more intolerant and violently persecuting of others, was to emerge later. Why an authoritarian tradition should have persisted for so long in the church is not obvious. The evidence of history suggests that power is rarely relinquished willingly.

Shakespeare's *King Lear* begins with an arrogant king who has lost sight of reality, playing at relinquishing his power. The king is an image of psychological blindness, just as later Gloucester is of physical blindness; but Shakespeare never explains how the king came to be so psychologically blind. Celebrated words of Lord Acton, a nineteenth-century historian and a Catholic who was opposed to the definition of papal infallibility, provide an explanation: 'Power tends to corrupt and absolute power corrupts absolutely.' Acton's words are, in effect, the statement of a psychological law; they suggest that popes, arriving at the papal throne as benevolent men, often become intolerant and dogmatic, seemingly as a consequence of possessing immense power.

History records that there have been many immoral popes, just as there have been many immoral cardinals and bishops. Psychology recognizes the importance of an organization such as the church being appropriately staffed by morally good people. But a social psychological account sees that evils done by popes, and those holding power in the church, are often inadequately explained in terms of their personalities. According to social psychology, it is less the sort of person you are, and more the sort of situation you are in, that decides how you think, feel and act. Church history confirms that popes, cardinals and bishops, however humble they might once have been, in office frequently become obsessed with their own authority and power. Social psychology explains evils done by the institutional church as often less a product of the personalities of those involved and related more to their positions of power within an authoritarian structure. Social psychology sees situations of immense power as especially fraught with danger, recognizing that possessing power without restraints and with minimum accountability is especially damaging psychologically. Acton's words express a law of human behaviour.

But, as Milgram's research reveals, the dangerous influence of power relates also to subordinates. Though the intolerance characterizing long periods of church history may partly have been a consequence of the authoritarian personalities of many ordinary Catholics, social psychology stresses the extent to which how we behave is a product of our situation; and ordinary Catholics have existed as subordinates within an authoritarian church. In hierarchical organizations which emphasize inequality and obedience to authority, subordinates too are changed and, as Milgram's research suggests, tend to feel less responsibility for their actions. Ordinary priests and people have been involved in past crimes of the church, such as persecution of Jews and heretics and supposed 'witches', in obedience to popes, cardinals, bishops and papal inquisitors. Milgram's research, demonstrating that in situations of hierarchical power we tend to obey the orders of authority regardless of their content, again locates the cause of the church's violent history in its authoritarian tradition.

There is a further, related cause of a persecuting authoritarian tradition within the church. For nearly fifteen hundred years the belief 'Outside the church there is no salvation' was part of the Catholic authoritarian tradition; from the early thirteenth century popes and church councils proclaimed this belief as central church doctrine. The psychological core of such a dogma is an assertion of difference, of a difference between ourselves and others, between us and them. Adorno's *The Authoritarian Personality* study and Rokeach showed that authoritarian and closed-minded people are very conscious of differences and tend to reject those different from themselves in some way. An authoritarian Catholic tradition has stressed difference between us and them – between us, insiders who are saved, and them, outsiders who are damned. This polarization into good and bad is psychologically significant, and in Jungian psychology symptomatic of not accepting one's shadow. The Catholic authoritarian tradition is characterized by a denial of the shadow.

This emphasis on difference, at its most extreme in past declarations of 'No salvation outside the church', but emerging also in papal statements contrasting the supposedly evil goings-on of the secular world with an idealized picture of the church, results from a refusal to accept the shadow. The superior moral tone of many encyclicals and church pronouncements, and the high moral ground claimed for themselves by popes and bishops, is symptomatic of a denial of the reality of their own and the church's shadow side. And because of projection that follows, denial of the shadow is dangerous; Jung stated that whatever is unconscious is projected. Jungian-inclined historians regard centuries of persecution by the Roman Catholic Church of Jews, non-believers, heretics and others as partly the result of the church's refusal to acknowledge its own shadow, and of subsequent projection.

Fairbairn's object-relations theory also regards emphasis on difference between us and them as symptomatic of denial and projection. According to object relations, the child is born psychologically whole. But in our early months and years, imperfect relationships with parents and other carers fragment the primal wholeness with which we are born. The wholeness and its subsequent fragmentation, located by object-relations theory at the beginning of every human life, is placed by Catholic tradition at the beginning of human history. The 1994 *Catechism of the Catholic*

Church holds that our wholeness was fragmented by the sin of our first parents, described in Genesis. In the traditional Catholic account, this fall consequent on the original sin of Adam and Eve destroyed an original harmony in human beings. But in the object-relations account, a *fall* occurs in every human life as the wholeness of the new-born infant, experiencing the imperfect relationships of the real world, splits and fragments.

Object relations holds that this original splitting not only creates personality but affects the subsequent workings of personality. When a relationship fails in adult life, we sometimes cope by mentally 'internalizing' the other person and indulging in a fantasy relationship. As babies, we do this all the time. Babies fantasize perfect relationships to compensate for unsatisfactory real-life relationships with parents and carers. As infants, in our internal fantasy world we obtain from mother or father – if only in fantasy! – the totally fulfilling relationship they fail to provide for us in the real external world. Of course, in our internal fantasy world there are no real people, only fantasy objects – hence the theory's title; in this internal world, the infant only has fantasy relationships with fantasy mothers and fathers and carers.

Fairbairn maintains that when infants internalize figures of real people, such as mother or father, these internalized fantasies become partly autonomous. If a father constantly rejects his baby son, the boy internalizes an image of father in order to have a 'satisfying' relationship with him – if only in fantasy. But the boy inevitably internalizes, with the image of father, the father's rejection and, as a consequence, the boy comes to see himself as rejected and worthless. The rejecting father now exists not only in the external world but also within the boy; the rejecting father is now part of his personality. Having internalized 'bad' aspects of real external people in order to control them, we create within ourselves what Fairbairn terms 'a fifth column of internal persecutors', similar to the Jungian shadow. The boy's personality is now split and contains semi-autonomous elements that reject him; as a result, he undervalues himself and feels there is something wrong with him.

With our self split by internalized 'objects', such as images of a cold mother or a belittling father, we are now confused as to which feelings are ours and which are the feelings of others. Is the coldness mine or my mother's, the belittling mine or my father's? A particular insight of object-relations theory is to see that internal images of parents, which eventually partly constitute our personality, may have little relation to what a parent is 'really' like. A child's image of mother as belittling, or the anger an infant sees in father, may be the child's own emotions projected out on to the parents. (Of course, the belittling or anger is not always the child's projection; real parents and other carers in the real external world clearly are sometimes angry, cold, rejecting, violent, belittling.)

By internalizing troubling faults and images of mother and father in the external world, which then become a 'fifth column of internal persecutors', the child, and later adult, creates an illusion of ideal parents. For example, a male infant might want a perfect relationship with his fantasy mother who, in real life, he experiences as cold. In order to have this ideal relationship he removes from his perception of her all that is unsatisfactory and nasty; he can then see his mother as wholly good. The result is idealization, and as an adult he will say of his 'real' mother in the external world, 'She is a saint'. But the 'bad mother' is now within him and has to be dealt with in some way.

And according to object-relations theory, we often deal with an 'internal persecutor', such as a 'bad mother', in the way that we deal with the Jungian shadow – by projection. We might see God as loving because of happy childhood relationships but, since relationships with parents are inevitably flawed, we might also emerge from childhood with unconscious negative images of our parents, which we project on to God. This might happen even though our unconscious images of, say, mother or father as rejecting and judgmental are, in part, originally projections of our own rejecting and judgmental feelings on to them.

Adults push negative feelings originating in infancy outwards; the 'bad mother' inside us is projected on to various other women, whom we then regard as ice maidens, whores, witches. In the past, the Catholic Church has labelled thousands of innocent women as evil witches and burnt them. But the 'evil' did not exist in the women; the 'evil' was a projection by popes, bishops, priests and laity of their own (in Fairbairn's account) 'fifth column of internal persecutors' and (in Jung's account) internal shadow.

At many periods of history, the church's attempt to rid itself of its 'internal persecutors' and shadow by projection has taken the form of demonization. The church has projected its negative side on to groups that the church felt threatened by, or to whom the church felt hostility, and then regarded the group as in some way possessed by the devil. Such groups were often held by the church literally to embody the devil. The church then used such demonization as a justification for violently persecuting or annihilating such groups. Authoritarian personalities, once they believe – as a result of demonization – that particular groups are less than human, feel that they can then perpetrate any violence on them. The Jewish people has constantly been a target for demonization by the church. From about the twelfth century, the papacy accused the Jews of having knowingly murdered God as agents of the devil.

Object-relations theory sees that we live in two worlds: we exist in the external world of real relationships with very human parents, imperfect friends, flawed colleagues, fallible popes. But we exist also in an internal world of 'relationships' with fantasy people, such as ideal or demon mothers and fathers. And from this internal world, we project on to the external world not only much of what is negative within us but also our idealizations. When we project out our fantasy idealizations, the result is saintly mothers, heroic fathers, godly bishops, infallible popes. An internal world, where we refuse to acknowledge our own 'internal persecutors' and our shadow, psychologically underpins the authoritarian tradition. And indicative of this denial of our 'internal persecutors' and shadow, and of consequent projection, is the emphasis on difference which characterizes the authoritarian tradition.

Object-relations theory sees this emphasis on difference and extreme contrasts – women as either witches and whores or madonnas and virgin saints – as symptomatic of psychological splitting. Through nearly fifteen hundred years, Catholics within the authoritarian tradition have projected their own 'internal persecutors' and shadow on to Jews; in his study *Vicars of Christ*, de Rosa reports that the institutional church published over a hundred antisemitic documents between the sixth and twentieth centuries. The Jews were then discriminated against and persecuted by the church, while popes and bishops idealized the church as spotless and perfect.

Denial and projection of shadow and 'internal persecutors' by an authoritarian church, often by demonizing what is outside, is invariably accompanied by idealization of what is inside. Pope, Curia, cardinals and bishops sense the 'evil' presence of shadow and 'internal persecutors' within their own personalities and the church. But they refuse to acknowledge that the violence, sexuality, anger, greed and hunger for power of unconscious shadow, and the negative 'internal persecutors', are really within themselves and the church. For much of Catholic history, the hierarchy of the church have projected their own unconscious shadow and 'internal persecutors' on to outside groups, such as heretics, reformers, Jews, non-Catholics generally, non-believers, women, alchemists, gay people; they have then persecuted such groups. Popes, cardinals and bishops, having split off and projected on to others their own and the church's shadow and 'internal persecutors', then idealize Catholicism and pronounce the church immaculate and perfect.

The Catholic liberal tradition, however, is not characterized by this polarization and emphasis on differences. Simone Weil had recognized the great truths contained in non-Christian religions long before the church's present limited ecumenism. The Catholic liberal tradition does not split humanity into us and them, insiders and outsiders, saved and damned. Catherine is said to have told Christ that she could never reconcile herself to the thought of a single person being lost from God. A liberal tradition stresses the unity and oneness of all human beings. The desire for universal reconciliation is central to the liberal tradition; psychologically such a desire partly relates to solving the problem of our own shadow and 'internal persecutors'.

The shadow, the demanding instinctive side of ourselves, a product of our passionate flesh-and-blood bodies, is seen by Jung as largely innate but added to by our life experiences; for Fairbairn, the 'fifth column of internal persecutors' is completely acquired. Both Jung and Fairbairn emphasize the great harm and damage done by projection, especially when we project the largely inborn shadow and our acquired 'internal persecutors' on to other people.

But though Jung stresses that there is immense danger while our shadow side remains unconscious, he sees the shadow made conscious as a vital power for good in our lives. Fairbairn here differs from Jung; Fairbairn holds that only bad objects exist in the unconscious. For Fairbairn, the solution is to struggle out of the persecuting internal world of bad objects into real human relationships. According to object-relations theory, the more we enter into contact and integration with people in the external world, the less disruptive are these bad internal objects. Fairbairn sees disruption of our personality and behaviour by this 'fifth column of internal persecutors' reduced and minimized by meaningful relationships with real people in the real world.

Object-relations theory would see Catholicism's recent ecumenism as resulting from Catholics, in modern pluralist societies, constantly meeting people of other Christian traditions and other religious faiths. The institutional church's past demonizing of non-Catholics and non-Christians could only be effective as long as the church was able to keep other religious traditions at a distance; in the Middle Ages and Renaissance, Jews were often segregated in ghettos. While contact and interaction with others was minimal, ordinary Catholics remained psychologically vulnerable to the church's demonizing portrayal of non-Catholics; as a result, Catholics tended to project their negative internal fantasies on to people of non-Catholic religious traditions. When Catholics, as a result of social changes, ceased to be apart from those in other religious traditions, they were no longer so susceptible to the church's demonizing portrayal of non-Catholics. In object-relations terms, Catholics experiencing real relations in the real world with people of other Christian traditions and other religious faiths withdrew their projections. The result is a more tolerant society, and ecumenism.

The authoritarian church's refusal to acknowledge its own shadow and 'internal persecutors' makes it difficult for ordinary Catholics to acknowledge their own negative side. 'There is need of people knowing about their shadow,' writes Jung in a letter to Father Victor White, a Catholic priest, 'because there must be

someone who does not project. They ought to be in a visible position where they would be expected to project and unexpectedly
they do not project! They can thus set a visible example which
would not be seen if they were invisible.' In the past, influenced
by an authoritarian hierarchy and institutional church, Roman
Catholics have often projected their shadow and 'internal persecutors' on to members of other Christian traditions and other faiths;
they have then felt hostile towards those on whom they have projected their own unconscious negative side.

Alcoholism among priests, the preoccupation with power of male
religious in schools and of priests in parishes, bullying by nuns in
children's homes, may originate partly from unconscious 'internal
persecutors' and shadow. An authoritarian Catholicism's condemnation of the 'flesh', and an authoritarian church's insistence on the
celibacy of the priesthood, possibly increases the difficulty of
recognizing and dealing with 'internal persecutors' and shadow.
Catholic liberal tradition, while stressing the importance of self-
control and of controlling our negative side, sees danger in the
Catholic authoritarian tradition's disregard and denial of unconscious factors.

Psychotherapists stress the danger for each of us of a lack of
insight into our own unconscious. Psychologists would regard the
famous Catholic guilt, and the intolerance and irritability which
characterizes those striving after excessive virtue, as caused partly
by an inability to come to terms with the more unconscious dimensions of our personality. Individuals within the Catholic liberal
tradition seem likely to be more loving and compassionate, partly as
a result of coming to terms with their shadow and 'internal persecutors' – expressed in Christian language as the acknowledgment that
'I am a sinner'.

Also central to the Catholic authoritarian tradition is the assertion that values and truths taught by the church exist in permanent
and unchanging form. The Catholic authoritarian tradition is characterized by hostility to change and development. Significantly,
Adorno's research revealed the rigid conservatism, the clinging to
'things as they are', of the authoritarian personality. In the Catholic
authoritarian tradition, an intense conservatism and adherence to

the past is characterized not only by hostility to change but by a denial that change is possible. The authoritarian tradition asserts that church teaching is definitive, final and unalterable. In the nineteenth century, Pope Pius IX condemned the idea that, as a result of growing human understanding, church teaching might be subject to development. The First Vatican Council subsequently declared that meaning given in the past by the church to dogmas must never be deviated from on the claim of a deeper understanding. In the present century, Pius X rejected the notion of any such development and required all Catholic priests to do so. But social psychology would expect change and development. In the Middle Ages, the church taught that charging interest on money loaned was morally wrong; popes firmly condemned such practice, termed usury. Loaning money at interest is now accepted by the church.

The dogma of the church from the thirteenth century, of 'No salvation outside the church', was confirmed by Pope Pius IX to be true church teaching as recently as the middle of the nineteenth century; but at the same time Pius IX significantly qualified the teaching. And in the twentieth century, a more liberal church has emphatically rejected such a teaching. Galileo and Darwin were condemned by the church partly because their views called in question a literal reading of scripture. Galileo was censured because his view that the earth circled the sun contradicted the suggestion in the Old Testament that the sun moved in relation to a stationary earth. Darwin's theory of evolution cast doubt on the Genesis account of God's creation of Adam and Eve. But a more liberal church can now accommodate Galileo and, to some extent, Darwin because of a changed view of scripture; the church now rejects a literal interpretation of the Old Testament. And with a further development in nineteen hundred years teaching, Roman Catholic orthodoxy now regards even the New Testament as sometimes requiring interpretation.

The church has also changed teaching in regard to the marriage act. With the exception of intercourse between a couple who are sterile or too old, in the past the church regarded as sinful, even in marriage, a sexual act not open to reproduction and where there was no intention of procreation. But since the middle of the twentieth century, the church has accepted as morally permissible regulating pregnancy by the natural 'safe period' method of birth control. And the church's present position, that the intention to avoid procreation is legitimate, reverses centuries of condemnation.

There has been a change from a married to a celibate priesthood; such a change was firmed up and imposed on a reluctant clergy by an increasingly authoritarian church in the middle of the twelfth century. A significant time in church history seems to have been the late twelfth century, by which time the growing power of the papacy had become almost absolute. Modern historians report that by the late twelfth century disobedience to the popes was regarded as heresy, to be eradicated by force.

From the start of the Christian era into the first half of the twelfth century, with certain exceptions in the third to sixth centuries, homosexuality seems to have been accepted by the church. Early medieval literature suggests that gay relationships, often between priests, were open and accepted. A recent study by Boswell revealed the existence of a tradition, within the church, of priests solemnizing same-sex unions in religious ceremonies paralleling heterosexual marriage services. Boswell's research recovered, from across the Christian world, manuscripts of ceremonies solemnizing same-sex unions dating from early in the Christian era; some manuscripts were as late as the sixteenth century. But by the late medieval period, the institutional Catholic Church had become intensely hostile to homosexuality. Boswell suggests that damaged surviving copies of same-sex ceremonies indicate that such documents were often destroyed during this period. The institutional church's change from acceptance to condemnation of homosexuality, and eventually to involvement in the persecution of those in gay relationships, began in the second half of the twelfth century.

But concurrent with the papacy's possession of almost total power within an authoritarian church by the late twelfth century, continuing through the centuries that followed, are the later Crusades, the early Inquisition, and increased persecution of Jews, of heretics such as the Albigensians and Waldenses, of early scientist-alchemists, of ordinary women as supposed witches, and of those not conforming to the pope's authority. By the fourteenth century, God or Catherine's projection on to God was declaring in the *Dialogue* that anyone who disobeyed the pope would go to hell. Social psychology would see the church's great intolerance and persecution, as the papacy's power increased through the Middle Ages and into the Renaissance, to be the product of the complete dominance of an authoritarian tradition within the institutional church.

By the nineteenth century the institutional church no longer had power over life and death, but what remained was psychological power, such as that of forgiving sins, of excommunication and of other forms of exclusion from the church; this remained a powerful source of control, claiming to carry the threat of God's punishment and damnation. In the nineteenth century, the papacy condemned human rights, social equality, freedoms of conscience and religious belief, maintaining time and again that such condemnations were based in authentic church teaching. But human rights, equality and basic freedoms are now accepted by the church and enshrined in the documents of the Second Vatican Council. The Catholic Church now even approves of democratic forms of government – except within the church!

A Catholic liberal tradition, while acknowledging the value of the past and of continuity, believes also in the validity of development. The liberal tradition recognizes that certain teachings exist that will not change, such as 'Love your neighbour' and 'Thou shalt not murder'. But the Catholic liberal tradition sees that many moral rules, regarded by the church as absolute and unalterable and God-given, are relative and the man-made creations of an authoritarian church. Many such rules are also man-made in being made by men and not women!

The Catholic liberal tradition recognizes that certain church teaching, once thought unchangeable, has simply changed. The Catholic liberal tradition regards church teaching as sometimes the product of the church working with imperfect knowledge at a certain period of history, and often shaped by the authoritarian values and structure of the church at that time; such teaching may need to be changed in the light of new knowledge, especially scientific knowledge. Certain such changes, such as the ordination of married men, would be a return to earlier practice; and Boswell's research suggests that the acceptance of gay and lesbian relationships as good and God-given would also be a return to an earlier tradition.

A liberal tradition holds that Catholic teaching, and development in teaching, should be the product not only of informed interpretation of revelation, but also of reason working within philosophy, theology and modern secular knowledge. Cardinal Newman referred to the church's three voices of tradition and authority, of theology and reason, and of the laity. The Catholic liberal tradition, in contrast to the authoritarian tradition where primarily the voice of authority is heard, stresses the value of teaching and of development in teaching founded ultimately on common agreement, rather than on the mere exercise of authority.

According to psychology, the authoritarian tradition's hostility to change and development, rather than being the result of certainty, is more likely the product of unadmitted uncertainty. A Catholic liberal tradition recognizes that an institutional church cannot provide absolute and definitive solutions; Catholics have to accept uncertainty and to tolerate ambiguity in their lives. The 'tolerance of ambiguity' referred to by psychologists and the 'negative capability' of Keats enable us to live with contradictions and mysteries. The authoritarian tradition's claim that the church's past and present teaching remains true for all time, and not open to development by deeper understanding, is probably caused psychologically by a craving for certainty and by difficulty with tolerating ambiguity. The Catholic liberal tradition recognizes the painful necessity of living with doubt, with the ambiguity of conflicting experiences, with unanswered and unanswerable questions, and with change and development.

And a central ambiguity tolerated within the Catholic liberal tradition is acknowledging the worth of not easily reconcilable values. A liberal Catholicism, while recognizing the value of a qualified conservatism, rejects a static view of truth and attempts to reformulate, in the light of new knowledge, teaching expressed in the thought of the past. A liberal Catholicism asserts the primacy of love and the free conscience over the claims of authority, at the same time acknowledging the necessity for dialogue between authority and the individual. A Catholic liberal tradition also attempts to live with the ambiguity of the opposing, and often irreconcilable, claims of hierarchy and equality.

A liberal tradition recognizes that human behaviour seems, in an intellectually irreconcilable way, both caused (by our biology, our past and our present) and free. But the Catholic liberal perspective, recognizing also the seeming incompatibility of justice and compassion, stresses the caused dimension in human behaviour and regards people with compassion rather than judgment. Julian of Norwich, as aware as any modern psychologist of the complexity of human intention and causation, regards human actions as usually a mixture of good and bad: 'For a man sees some deeds as good and some deeds as evil, but our Lord God does not see them so.'[3]

Christ directs us to concern ourselves with the plank in our own eye (psychologically, our own shadow and 'internal persecutors'), rather than with the speck in other people's eyes (psychologically, our projection). Influenced by psychology, the Catholic liberal tradition sees that if, as Catholics, we make more conscious the shadow and 'internal persecutors' within ourselves and project them less, we become less judgmental of others. And history would suggest that those with authority in the church, such as popes, cardinals and bishops, have a particular need to make more conscious and project less their own shadows and 'internal persecutors'. A liberal Catholic Church, psychologically more self-aware, would be less judgmental of others, more compassionate and more loving.

Simone Weil, as a Jew, would have known of the Catholic Church's persecution of the Jewish people over many, many centuries. She knew also of the violence constantly done by the institutional church to heretics, pagans and generally to any who did not conform to church authority. Simone believed that if the Catholic Church was to make a significant contribution to the world, rather than be just a large parochial organization, the institutional church would have to declare publicly that it had changed or wished to. 'Otherwise who could take her seriously when they remembered the Inquisition,'[4] she says in *Waiting on God*.

In recent times the institutional church has begun to express sorrow for past evils done by the church such as the persecution of the Jews, the Crusades and the Inquisition. Church reports on the causes of such evils assume that their causes are to be found in the bygone and buried past; and the institutional church has certainly changed in many ways. But psychology suggests that such crimes were partly a product of the church's authoritarianism; and a psychological perspective recognizes that the contemporary church remains characterized even now by many features of the authoritarian tradition responsible for such crimes in the past.

Toward the end of his life, Karl Rahner, the twentieth-century Catholic theologian, writes with Karl-Heinz Weger: 'Good news? Joy? The freedom of the children of God? It would be hard to say that the documents of the Church's teaching authority exude a spirit of freedom and joy. What do we expect from Rome except prohibitions and condemnations!' (*Our Christian Faith*). Psychology and the four women would seem to suggest that we would hear more of the good news, and a greater spirit of freedom and joy would be present, in a church more influenced by its liberal tradition.

5

Psychological Growth

For in our mother Christ we profit and grow.

(Julian of Norwich, *Revelations of Divine Love*)

But it is obvious that the values of women differ very often from the values which have been made by the other sex . . . Yet it is the masculine values that prevail.

(Virginia Woolf, *A Room of One's Own*)

No man is an island, entire of itself.

(John Donne, *Revelations*)

A man of forty-five is not the same person that he was at twenty-five but only older. Developmental psychologists, such as Erik Erikson, hold that at forty-five he differs in significant ways from the person he was at twenty-five. Life, according to developmental psychology, is a series of stages. And developmental psychologists maintain that as stages change, our personality needs to develop to meet these changes. Erikson would regard a woman of fifty-five who is psychologically no different from when she was thirty-five as delayed in her development. He sees human beings as needing to live their lives in a continuous state of development.

Like Freud, Erikson sees the first stages of life as shaping personality and influencing the rest of our lives. Erikson emphasizes the importance in these early stages of our relationship with parents, regarding feeding and toilet training as particularly significant areas of parent-child interaction. But in infancy and childhood, parents and other carers express relationships also through their presence, physical contact, play, teaching the child skills and through sharing tasks at home or school. What children at this stage learn through relationships is their own way of relating to others, independence, trust, shame, control, guilt. They also acquire ways of coping with continuity and change; if in our adult years as Catholics we chase after the new, completely disregarding church tradition, or if we cling to past church teaching, fearful of innovation, this is partly because of our early experiences.

But Erikson, an ego psychologist in the psychoanalytic tradition, holds that important psychological experience and development also happen after childhood. For example, he sees success or failure in coping with sexuality during teenage years as affecting, for better or worse, the sexuality of adulthood and middle age. And he argues that personality, though largely formed by childhood, can subsequently be altered by our conscious thinking ego – if only slightly. He particularly asserts that damage done in childhood or any early stage can be repaired at a later time; for example, mistrust caused by clumsy parenting in infancy may be remedied in later years by a caring teacher or by a partner in marriage. It is never too late, in Erikson's view, to remedy damage done in earlier stages. But he holds that later influences can also work negatively; the effects of good early relationships, though normally lasting, may be harmed by subsequent experience, such as the death of a loved one.

Erikson sees one particular task of development existing at all stages – that of balancing our need for relationships and our need for independence. Children attempt to achieve this balance in regard to parents and siblings. Adolescents struggle very obviously both to enjoy intimacy with others and to find a separate identity. Throughout adulthood, men and women strive, in areas of their lives such as sexual love, to attain a balance of intimacy with others and autonomy. But Erikson reports, as Freud had done earlier, that women and men appeared to seek a different balance: women were usually less obsessed than men with achieving independence and valued intimate relationships more highly than men did.

Freud had stated that the unconscious conscience, which he called the superego, was different in men and women. He reported that the superego was not 'so inexorable, so impersonal' in women as in men. Strangely, Freud took this as evidence that women were inferior! He concluded that women, because they were less inexorable and impersonal, 'show less sense of justice than men'.

Freud, though recognizing the importance of human relationships, seemed not to see any value in placing relationships above rules and, as a consequence, being less judgmental of others. Christ clearly saw such a value. Before the woman taken in adultery he addresses a crowd of *men*: Let him who is without sin cast the first stone. Julian in her *Revelations* records God as loving, but not judging, human beings.

Erikson's contrasting needs, for relationships and independence, appear linked to two groups of human values that anthropologists and psychologists have found contrasted in many cultures. Centring upon the need for relationships is a valuing of intimacy, feelings, compassion and caring for others. The second group of values, linked to what Erikson sees as the need for independence, emphasizes separateness, personal assertion and power; here intellect and logic are regarded as of particular importance.

Jungian psychology associates the first group with the 'feminine' side of the human self, which Jung terms the 'anima', and the second group with the 'masculine' side of the self, which Jung terms the 'animus'. In the past, Western society has linked the two groups of values to women and men. Certainly, in the past, anima qualities seem more often to have characterized women, and animus qualities seem more to have characterized men. But the extent to which innate biology makes anima qualities more typical of women and animus qualities more typical of men is much debated. Some argue that biology plays a part. But most psychologists recognize also the role of society and culture in shaping men and women differently; here again, the child's experience in the family is central.

Psychologists hold that what happens in families is usually different for boys and for girls. In the past women have been largely responsible for child-care; to a large extent they still are. Nancy Chodorow saw important consequences in mothers usually having been the adult to whom children were closest: growing-up for a girl is to become like mother, but for a boy growing-up involves becoming different and separate from mother. Girls, identifying with mother, experience being female in terms of a relationship with mother and do not need to separate to become women. Boys see becoming a man in terms of separation from mother; in addition, boys grow up more accustomed to the distant and more separate relationship experienced with father.

Chodorow sees the outcome of this childhood experience is that a boy matures maintaining boundaries between himself and others, finding intimacy threatening because his identity relates to his being independent and separate; in contrast, a girl matures with her identity related to the care of others and to intimate relationships, finding independence difficult, since she sees herself largely in terms of relationships with others. One consequence, Chodorow concludes, is that girls emerge from childhood better able than boys to feel sympathy and empathy for others, and valuing such qualities more than boys.

Earlier relevant research on childhood was done by Piaget. Watching children at play, he noted that boys and girls had different attitudes to rules. Piaget records that boys were fascinated by rules, often appearing to enjoy arguments about rules as much as the game itself. He found that girls had less interest than boys in rules as such, regarding them in a more relaxed and pragmatic way, and were generally more flexible about rules. Girls seemed much happier to change rules and to make exceptions to them than boys were. Girls, Piaget observed, seemed extremely tolerant about rule infringements, whereas boys emphasized more the obligation to obey rules.

The different attitudes of girls and boys to rules observed by Piaget led him to state that 'the legal sense is far less developed in little girls than in boys'. He writes that when girls play games together they make up fewer rules than boys; and girls never codify or organize these rules as much as boys do. We might conclude from this and other findings of Piaget that girls are less legalistic and obsessively rule-bound than boys. But Piaget regards what he calls 'the legal sense' as central to moral development. So, like Freud, he rather oddly considers his research as evidence for less moral development in girls than boys. But Julian's God, like Piaget's girls, is also 'far less developed' on 'the legal sense', seemingly less interested in the rules of life and less exacting about whether they are obsessively obeyed. Julian's God, like Piaget's girls, is more concerned with the welfare of the players who participate.

The present response of the Catholic Church to marriage breakdown illustrates the extent to which, like Piaget's boys, the church is preoccupied with rules. Catholics whose marriages have failed are now applying for church annulments in greatly increased numbers; the church is now granting many annulments. But the institutional church attempts to maintain the permanence of marriage as an absolute rule. The church does this by granting many marriage annulments on the grounds that a marriage never occurred in the first place. A reason typically given is the couple's psychological unreadiness for marriage, usually described in terms of defectiveness in their original consent. By granting annulments on the grounds that there never was a marriage, the church keeps intact the permanence of marriage as an absolute rule.

Couples often resent an annulment in terms which declare to them, and to their children, that they were never really married. Some Catholics, seeking annulment of a marriage that failed after several years, reject annulments granted in these terms. They often do so because such an annulment is legislating out of existence a relationship that, before foundering, may have contained love and commitment and been blessed by children loved by both parents. The terms of such a proposed annulment do not accord with the couple's experience, which is that there was once a marriage, but something went wrong and the marriage did not prove permanent. Having rules, to which there can be no exceptions, seems psychologically important for the church's male hierarchy.

But research, such as that of Piaget and others, suggesting certain qualities to be more typical of women and other qualities to be more characteristic of men, often does not explain the origins of these differences. And psychologists recognize that, however such differences between women and men might originate, they are reinforced in Western society by adult culture. Western society, having shaped women to be 'feminine' and men to be 'masculine', has then proclaimed 'masculine' values to be superior. Jung believed that anima values associated with women had been consistently undervalued in Western culture. Even early in the present century Virginia Woolf had no doubts which values still dominated.

From the twelfth century, when marriage was forbidden for priests in the Western Church, the celibate male has been held up to

Catholics as an ideal. The Roman Catholic Church, in the formation of priests and religious, has since emphasized independence more than relationships, detachment above intimacy, intellect rather than feelings and has stressed obedience to rules. In some male religious orders, such as the Jesuits, training in the past has aimed at forming an autonomous priestly personality, a monastery in the world but not of the world. The Catholic training of male religious seems to have been in danger of making a Nietzschean superman independence into a sort of Christian ideal.

The vow of obedience, taken by Catholic religious, psychologically tends to complement this emphasis on independence. An obsession with obedience characterizes the authoritarian personality, who values the detachment and separateness of obedience above intimate relationships between equals. To compensate for an obsequious obedience to superiors, authoritarian personalities assert their independence by dominating subordinates.

The emphasis that Catholicism has placed on such animus or 'masculine' values, particularly for its celibate clergy, seems strange; a preoccupation with independence and separation from others, and a stress on intellect, authority and obedience to rules, does not appear particularly Christian. In contrast, the more anima or 'feminine' emphasis on empathy and sympathy, on intimate connectedness with others, on caring for others and on relationships rather than rules, does seem essentially Christian. The basic Christian ethic, Love your neighbour as yourself, is wholly about relationships; and Christianity has always regarded loving God and our neighbour as the purpose of human life. Catherine regarded the Christian Trinity, three persons in one God, as signifying that the uncreated Love at the centre of our existence is, or involves, a relationship.

Jung always esteemed highly the values of what he termed the anima. He argued that Western culture undervalued anima qualities and dangerously exaggerated the worth of animus values. But Jung held that women and men need both animus and anima to become whole. According to Jungian psychology, within every woman exists an animus, an unconscious 'masculine' side, and within every man exists an anima, an unconscious 'feminine' side; and the human self is whole only when both are incorporated. But a historical past in which anima qualities were regarded as more appropriate for women, and where animus qualities were regarded as more appropriate for men, has constricted the development of both women and men. As a consequence, many women have grown to adulthood having difficulty acknowledging certain needs within themselves, such as to be independent and separate and appropriately assertive; and many men have grown to adulthood with difficulty in recognizing certain needs within themselves, such as for caring relationships, for intimacy and connectedness with others, and for compassion. Jung stresses that both types of needs exist in both women and men; in Jungian psychology, to become whole a woman must incorporate her animus side and a man must incorporate his anima side.

It is quite possible that anima and animus values relate only historically to women and men. Social psychologists have noted that, influenced by the women's liberation movement, there seems to be some convergence in the personalities of women and men. Anima and animus might simply express what is unfulfilled in men and in women because of the different demands that society has made on them in the past. What psychologists, such as Jung, have diagnosed is a polarity which, when seen by a society in terms of female and male, constrains psychological development in both men and women.

Though development psychologists now recognize both sides of the polarity as essential for all human beings, within the Catholic Church there seems a cultural lag. A central element in this polarity are the contrasting needs of human beings for both personal relationships and independence. But the training of priests and nuns has usually emphasized animus qualities of independence and individual autonomy, and usually still does. A need for intimate relationships in priests or nuns has been, and still is, regarded by bishops and religious superiors as a sign of immature dependency. But the part played by close friendships in convents is further evidence of this need for intimacy. And the extent of sexual relationships, heterosexual and gay, among nominally celibate priests confirms developmental psychology's assertion of the need for personal and caring relationships among men.

But what seems to emerge from Jung, Erikson, Freud, Chodorow and Piaget are differences in human development which have been associated with women and men. The psychological development characterized by qualities such as relationships and intimacy, where women have traditionally been located, will in the following discussion be referred to as the relating stage. The psychological development characterized by qualities such as independence and separateness, where men traditionally have been located, will be referred to as the independent stage. We will refer to the stage of development beyond the polarity as the interpersonal self.

Adults at the independent stage of development are preoccupied, as the boys were in Piaget's research, with rules. It is possible that the priest-lawyers of the Roman Curia who, motivated by a preoccupation with rules, add to the church's thousand or so canon laws, are fixated at the independent stage. People at the independent stage, troubled by the untidiness of life and of feelings in particular, invariably attempt to impose order; the need to be in control generally, and to be in charge with people, suggests that the individual in an extreme form of the independent stage has kinship with the authoritarian personality. The main concern of those at this stage of development is to discover the one correct solution to any problem and one correct set of rules. In contrast, God in the *Dialogue* tells Catherine that she would be mistaken in wanting 'to force all my servants to walk by the same path you yourself follow, for this would be contrary to the teaching given you by my Truth'.[1]

For those whose self remains at the independent stage, personal identity is seen in terms of achievements, abstract concepts, rules, principles. As a result, they feel threatened and on the defensive when their views are questioned, which they experience as an attack on their very self. Such a reaction is often characteristic of higher authority within the Catholic Church, where proposals for change, no matter how well argued, or how modest, may be condemned with excessive and disproportionate hostility.

At the independent stage, achieving personal autonomy is central, and emotional life and human relationships are subordinated. Those whose selfs remain firmly located in the independent stage, historically mostly men, fear emotional involvement and being loved; they find intimacy threatening. Now most psychologists hold, like Jung, that this typically male emphasis on qualities such as independence is one-sided and co-exists with an equally basic need, less acknowledged by men, for relationships and connectedness with others. Nevertheless, achieving personal autonomy and becoming separate from others, which the independent stage emphasizes, remain a necessary element in human development.

At the relating stage of development, personal identity is seen not in separation from others but in intimate and caring relationships; at this stage, being in relationships with others is more important than enforcing rules, just as it was for the girls in Piaget's research. Those whose development remains at the relating stage, historically usually women, attempt to resolve problems so that everyone can follow their conscience, and no one is hurt or excluded. Moral rules are acknowledged at this stage, but people at the relating stage stress compassion and the continual need to make exceptions. Julian in the *Revelations* sees God as more concerned with loving and caring for us than with checking that we keep the rules and with judging us when we fail to do so. Julian may have seen what development psychology now recognizes, that we are more likely to develop not when someone continually criticizes us but when someone accepts us as we are.

For those whose development is at the relating stage, a solution where no one gets hurt is more important than insisting that all the rules are kept. The self at the relating stage invariably stresses sympathy and empathy with others in seeking a solution to any problem. Tolerance is involved, since what matters is that no one should end up excluded or alone; Julian's God wanted no one left out. And Simone Weil, like many Christians, found particularly abhorrent the Catholic exclusion of the rest of humanity in its past teaching, 'Outside the church there is no salvation'. Catherine of Siena is said to have told Christ that she could never reconcile herself to the possibility of anyone being lost to God.

The relating stage of development is of immense value, embodying the Christian emphasis on relationships. Psychologically, its limitation is in locating our identity solely in relationships with others and in what others expect of us. The psychological weakness of the self at the relating stage is that, finding our self only in relationships, we never achieve a true separate identity. And if our self lacks appropriate separation and independence, we cannot truly relate because in our associations with others we will tend to fuse with them. Genuine relationships and true intimacy require an independent identity, which the self at the relating stage does not completely possess.

Women are likely to develop only as far as the relating stage in societies where they have no significant power. Until recently, in Western society the reality of women's position has been that men have political authority, exert control over women and make the significant decisions. It remains the reality of women's position within the Catholic Church. In Catholicism, what would be seen as legitimate independence and self-assertion in priest or layman would be regarded as selfishness in a woman and, particularly, in a nun. Thérèse of Lisieux seems a young women shaped by a society and convent life where her own needs are entirely subordinate to those of others. But what eventually emerges in Thérèse's auto-biography is her achievement, against all the odds, of personal independence.

Human development arrives at a greater wholeness when relating and independent stages combine in an interpersonal self. When women and men achieve the interpersonal self, they exist in genuine relationships with others and not in the isolation of the independent stage. Genuine intimacy with others is possible because we have achieved, at the interpersonal self stage, an appropriate personal autonomy which does not separate us from others. Women and men who have attained an interpersonal self do not – as at the relating stage – fuse with others in their relationships; possessing genuine selfs, they are truly able to relate to others and are capable of the intimacy possible in human relationships between people who have their own identities.

Though the input of the independent stage into the interpersonal self brings the awareness of the significance of rules, men and women possessing an interpersonal self know that people are more important than particular rules. The interpersonal self acknow-ledges that absolute and unchanging rules do exist – we should love and care for others; we should especially love and care for children; we should love and care for our parents; we should be compassionate and especially love and care for the sick, the poor, the old, the vulnerable; we should be just in our relations with others; we should not exploit others; we should not betray a trust, especially where a committed sexual or other deep relationship exists . . . Anthropological research indicates that such rules and principles are found among humans everywhere and throughout history; following these rules and putting these principles into practice takes different forms in different societies. But the interpersonal self, having incorporated the relating stage, recognizes that absolute rules which do exist are few, general and, significantly, about caring human relationships. The relating stage inputs into the interpersonal self the all-pervasiveness of one rule, to love our neighbour.

Catholicism's obsessive preoccupation with many rules is probably a consequence of members of the church hierarchy failing to incorporate the relating stage into their psychological development. Those at the independent stage of development derive moral rules solely from abstract principles, without consideration of the authentic experience of human beings and the reality of people as they are. The church in the past has condemned intercourse without the intention of procreation and still regards using artificial methods of birth-control as sinful; but married couples experience sexual intercourse, unrelated to any intention of procreation, as important for their relationship. Similarly, in recent times church rules have condemned same-sex relationships; but the experience of gay men and lesbians is of the goodness of genital same-sex relationship in expressing genuine and committed love. Popes, bishops and theologians, who have failed to incorporate relating stage values in their psychological development, are likely to create abstract rules damaging to people.

The interpersonal self recognizes the importance of human connectedness and relationships. The interpersonal self does not relativize principles but aims to have rules related to real life and starting from where human beings are. According to the interpersonal self, as far as possible rules should exclude no one; and, since people are more important than rules, there should always be compassion for those who cannot keep the rules. 'So I saw that Christ has compassion on us because of sin,'[2] says Julian.

Thérèse's autobiographical manuscripts can be read as an account of a growth to an interpersonal self. She moves from an independent stage preoccupation with rules made by other people to acquiring her own perspectives. Central to her development is a relating stage concern for others: 'A word, an amiable smile, often suffice to make a sad soul bloom.'[3] Thérèse anticipates modern psychology in recognizing that both independence and relationships are central to human development. Her life and writings counsel that no one should be dominated or controlled, whether by another person's authority or by impersonal rules. And the growth of Thérèse's relationships with others seem related to her own growth in a sense of self-worth. She sees spiritual development as related and connected to relationships of equality and interdependence. And Thérèse, believing that God needs her own and everyone's love, sees even our relationship with God as characterized by equality and mutual dependence.

Though the goal for both women and men is the wholeness of the interpersonal self, where they start from has, historically, usually been different. Women have been channelled by society into a relating stage where they are responsible for others, such as children and the elderly; it is here, usually, that women's journey to the interpersonal self begins. But typically, though women are expected to care for others, no one seems expected to care for them; this breeds resentment. Older Catholics have noticed that nuns who help and support priests are often unkind to other nuns in the convent. A significant development for a woman, at the relating stage, begins with the realization that she has as much need to be cared for as anyone else. In the past, certainly in the Catholic past, a woman has been taught to regard a concern for herself as selfish. So for a woman, development to the interpersonal self usually involves augmenting her relating stage concern for relationships, and for the care of others, with an independent stage awareness that she too has the right, as well as need, to be a cared-for individual with her own space. Psychologists, and women, now recognize that Christ's command to 'love our neighbour as ourself' requires that we love ourselves also.

Historically men have been channelled into the independent stage. So, for men, psychological development often involves moving from an emphasis on the abstractions of rules to a greater concern, acquired in human relationships, with the reality of the situations of individual people. The young celibate priest, emerging from a seminary where separateness and abstract principles have been stressed, is likely to be at the independent stage. But in the life of the parish he experiences other people's pain, such as that of divorced men and women hoping to remarry, and of couples who, already with several children, wish to use artificial methods of birth control condemned by the pope. Such an experience may move him beyond the moral abstractions taught in the seminary. The seminarian's 1994 *Catechism of the Catholic Church* tends to ignore, in a way no caring mother would, the specifics that affect real people in the real world, such as their biological make-up, individual histories and personal situations.

It is the specifics of real human beings, rather than general rules, which engage those at the relating stage. Confronted by suffering people, some priests change, becoming less preoccupied with the abstractions of their seminary textbooks – though they cannot admit this in public. Such priests are not selling out on morality; they are modifying, augmenting or even replacing with another moral perspective the teachings of a church fixated at the independent stage of development. Some priests come to reject an exclusively rule-based approach; they operate instead, or also, in terms of a morality based on relationships, concern for others and compassion. In the past the church has stressed the importance of compassion in the ministry of priests.

If priests at the independent stage do develop psychologically to an interpersonal self, they invariably acquire a relating stage realization of the limited value of rules. And since with an interpersonal self they no longer – as at the independent stage – regard their identities largely in terms of the rules taught them in the seminary, such priests are able to reflect critically on these rules. Such priests also recognize that where rules are valid, their implementation needs to be tempered by compassion. The effect of compassion may result in making a decision in terms of a greater good than that embodied in a specific rule; compassion sometimes involves opting for the lesser of two evils or attempting to emerge from a situation with the least possible damage done to those involved. In the *Dialogue*, God tells Catherine we are not to think of our sins without, at the same time, considering God's great love and mercy. Often only when working in a parish, exposed to the pain of others, does a priest begin to recognize that love and compassion, and not the rules of an authoritarian and patriarchal church, are central to Christian life.

Clearly, psychological development leading to such a recognition does not always occur. Celibate priests are isolated by their training and sometimes have few close relationships; the emphasis of their training and situation leads to separateness and an impersonal independence. As a result, they might come to experience the world of intimate and caring relationships as threatening. Such priests tend to remain at the independent stage, fail to develop an interpersonal self, and cope with their lives and work by stressing rules and regulations.

For both men and women to grow to the wholeness of an interpersonal self, incorporating both the relating and independent stages, society and culture have to recognize the value of such psychological development and provide support that makes this possible. Within secular society, this would appear to be beginning. But the Catholic Church, rather than encouraging growth to an interpersonal self, seems to stress still that the development of women remains within the relating stage, and the imposition of celibacy keeps many priests fixed in the independent stage.

The centrality of the interpersonal self emerges in Fairbairn's theory of object relations, sometimes referred to as interpersonal relations theory. Fairbairn says that human beings seek psychological security, achieving this when they maintain themselves as separate individuals in meaningful personal relationships. According to object-relations theory, such psychological security and wholeness involves a balance between dependence on others and independence. Fairbairn sees a deep human need for interdependence, which he characterizes as a mature dependency based in adult relationships. Catherine of Siena comments in the *Dialogue* that God has made us so that we need each other. Fairbairn regards psychological development as a growth from relationships of infantile dependency to mature dependence centred in adult relationships.

As Catholics, adult in years, we might – in our reverence for words from the pulpit and our uncritical acceptance of papal pronouncements – still be children at the infantile dependency stage. The Catholic who identifies completely and, so to speak, fuses with the pope and the institutional church, remains at this infantile stage. For Fairbairn, infantile dependency, characterized by identification and fusion with others, particularly with mother, is appropriate only in children. True psychological growth results in the child knowing who he or she is and realizing that mother is different. Object-relations theory maintains that as we grow older, each of us needs to move to mature dependency, where a certain separateness makes possible and enhances genuine and intimate relationships with others. But, object-relations theory emphasizes, mature dependence means that the independence traditionally regarded as so important, particularly by men, has to be balanced against the value of proper connectedness with others. Fairbairn stresses that people need relationships and do not seek some exaggerated independence in their lives.

Many characteristics of the institutional church make growing beyond infantile dependency difficult for Catholics; among them are the church's preoccupation with its own power and authority, its extreme hierarchical structure, an emphasis on obedience to its rules, fear as a way of enforcing obedience, antipathy to personal conscience and hostility to equality within the church. But new opportunities for growth are beginning to be offered by secular society; as a result, women and men are more able to move towards the wholeness of the interpersonal self, particularly in a better balance of the relating and independent stages, in a journey through childhood, young and mature adulthood, and middle age.

Jung sees the arrival of middle age as accompanied by the unsettling realization, at some level, that the way we have been regarding the world is no longer relevant. He writes of not being able to live the second half of life according to our programme for the first half. The way we see things will have changed radically, and our first-half-of-life programme will prove not to be adequate.For Jung, the beginning of middle age is often characterized by a sort of disorient-ation and crisis; the prodigal son's problems of sexuality and hedon-ism are added to or replaced by those of the dutiful but bitter and disappointed elder brother. The symptoms famously are depres-sion, anger, boredom, a nameless dread, sometimes disturbing sexuality, usually a desire for something more in life, a feeling that life has no meaning, a search for purpose, and an awareness of the inevitability of death. (Enough to get anyone down!) And according to developmental psychology, middle age usually increases the perennial human need both for independence and for intimacy in relationships. What Jungian psychology sees happening at middle age is the emergence of new forces from the unconscious.

Developmental psychologists recognize that some mid-life troubles are unfinished business, unresolved problems from earlier years returning, hopefully, this time to be resolved. For example, mothers and fathers might find that unresolved conflicts from the past, related to sexuality or to becoming independent of their own parents, return when a son or daughter enters puberty or leaves home. However, for Jung, the mid-life crisis is also a kind of second adolescence, where we attempt to find values to live by in the second half of life.

Just as ways in which we have coped until now with life prove generally unsatisfactory, so our past ways of relating to God become inadequate. A danger at mid-life is that our convictions harden and we become intolerant. With Catholics there is a danger of increasing dogmatism in our beliefs, of placing more emphasis on rigid rules, and of becoming bitterly critical of other people. As Catholics, we might in the earlier part of our lives have practised our religion as conventional believers.

Developmental psychology provides mid-life Catholics with the insight that we may have been attempting to use our Catholicism as a defence. We had believed our prayers, dutiful mass attendance, rosaries and obedience to the church would insulate us from the worst of life; but they have failed to do so. There has been much disappointment and pain in our own lives. Loved ones have suffered calamities or died, and all our Catholic beliefs seem not to have lessened our grief, anger, distress. If we remain now at the level of merely abiding by the rules of the church, we seem liable to become bitter, harsh, judgmental. Our increased dogmatism might be an attempt to conceal, and compensate for, uncertainty resulting from the failure of our earlier naïve Catholicism, which we had thought would protect us and enable us to keep control. According to developmental psychology, mid-life enables us to see that we are not, and never were, in control.

Simone Weil stresses the importance of recognizing the reality of our not being in control of our lives. She regards the universe, with its many millions of stars and galaxies, as revealing not God's power but God's renunciation of power. She holds that throughout our lives we need to abandon ourselves to God in a letting-go which is an imitation of God's own renunciation of power. But Simone emphasizes that our abandonment to God involves not the renunciation of control over our lives, since we never had any, but the renunciation of the illusion of our having power and control. She believed that affliction and suffering may work throughout our lives to destroy any such illusion.

Thérèse, too, though only twenty-four when she died, emphasized this need for letting-go. For Thérèse, there is both a passive and active dimension to our lives, the active element emerging in doing God's will in everyday events. But she sees spiritual growth as requiring also a passive element, which consists in relinquishing this notion of being in control, by surrendering our will to God. For Thérèse, what is important is not what happens to us, but the letting-go of our self to God in life's events.

A Christian psychology regards the New Testament journey to Emmaus as a metaphor for the mid-life crisis – and its resolution. The two disciples can see no way ahead because the enterprise they were engaged in with Christ seems, with the crucifixion, to have ended in failure. But on the way to Emmaus they meet Jesus; they do not recognize him at first, but when he reveals himself as the risen Christ they find a new purpose in their lives. A Christian psychology holds that for Christians the resolution to the mid-life crisis arrives when they find a new centre in Christ. Jung speaks of the problems of later life as being spiritual as much as psychological, and religious writers have talked of a second conversion.

Developmental psychology sees the resolution of the mid-life crisis as involving gratitude and appreciation for what we have had, and have achieved, in our lives. Psychologists recognize that middle age invites us to greater realism about ourselves; middle age invites us to an abandonment of now unrealizable ambitions, as well as to grief and mourning for what we have missed out on or have lost, such as youth. This makes the mid-life crisis a sort of death. The image of death and rebirth, of dying to rise again, so central to Christianity, as well as to the whole process of psychological development, is particularly relevant at mid-life.

Psychologists hold that resolving the problems of middle age involves acceptance – of our future death, of past pain, of injury caused us by events in our life, of damage done to us by other people and of damage that we ourselves have done to others. Julian asserts that whatever our past mistakes, we know that God, the good mother, allowed them because she wished us to have opportunities to learn for ourselves. 'A mother may sometimes let her child fall,' says Julian, 'and be unhappy in many ways for its own good. But she will never allow any real harm to come to the child, because of the love she bears it.'[4] For the individual Catholic, acceptance might also involve forgiving a frequently unloving and judgmental institutional church.

Developmental psychology also sees the resolution of the mid-life crisis as involving another sort of acceptance, an acceptance of the less attractive features of ourselves, such as the Jungian shadow and Fairbairn's internal persecutors; we need to recognize and acknowledge our destructive as well as our creative side. Jung holds that from such acceptance there emerges a wholeness and a new purpose and meaning in life. For many of us, the mid-life crisis might never be fully solved, and we continue with an unresolved dimension to our lives, like a damaged ship limping to its journey's end.

Secular and Christian liberal psychology agree that whatever wholeness emerges, as mid-life ends and old age begins, derives from acceptance and from an awareness of the goodness within our self. In Christian thought, the resolution of mid-life also involves achieving a sense of ourselves as persons made in God's image and loved by God. God cares about us constantly, says Julian, 'even while we are in sin'.[5] The Christian perception attempts to make some sense of our existence in the light of Christ's life, particularly since his life ended in death and apparent failure. And both a secular and Christian liberal psychology see resolution, in middle and old age, as emerging in a wisdom where we experience the imperfection of our life not as failure but as an imperfect work accepted with serenity.

According to Erikson, the central issue of mature age, the final stage of life, is overcoming despair by finding a certain integrity in the face of the death now close to us. He asserts that whether or not we realize it, we have at some level been reviewing our life. Erikson records that whatever satisfaction we might have with what has been achieved, we are likely to be troubled still by unfulfilled ambitions and by missed, never-to-return opportunities. They need to be acknowledged and accepted; otherwise, says Erikson, we despair. Rembrandt's self-portraits in old age seem to express acceptance and even – in spite of the anticipation of death in their record of the body's decay – affirmation. According to Erikson, confronted by death's approach we need to balance a sense of being, partly through an awareness of what we have been, against the reality of soon not being; the outcome of the right balance is wisdom.

Erikson and other developmental psychologists recognize that as we age the need for renunciation becomes even more pressing; in such renunciation we choose to relinquish what eventually in the final letting-go of death we have no choice about surrendering. In Christian thought, the end of our lives also involves replacing any remaining illusion of control with conscious trust and abandonment in our relationship to God.

6

Catholic Patriarchy

A woman's place is in the wrong.

(Old joke)

As truly as God is our father, so, just as truly, God is our mother.

(Julian of Norwich, *Revelations of Divine Love*)

I feel in me the *vocation* of the PRIEST. With what love, O Jesus, I would carry You in my hands when, at my voice, You would come down from heaven. And with what love would I give You to souls!

(Thérèse of Lisieux, *Story of a Soul*)

Until quite recently, most Christians took literally the story of Adam and Eve and the Fall in the Garden. Tempted by the serpent, Eve eats fruit from the forbidden tree and persuades Adam to do so. As a result, they are cast out of paradise; pain, sickness and death enter the world, and God makes Eve subject to her husband. There are no doubts about this God being male; he believes a man needs to be in charge!

According to my Catholic school, Adam was the head of the human race, and if Eve had failed to persuade him and she alone had eaten the apple, there would have been no fall. This is a marvel of sexist ingenuity. It would seem difficult to hold the woman responsible for the ensuing tragedy without crediting her with a certain authority. But the myth manages to do this, since the woman is regarded as the guilty party and largely to blame, but only the man is held to possess legitimate power. A patriarchal agenda, according to which women are held to be inferior to men and only what men do is important, characterizes much of Roman Catholic history. This agenda is not confined to the Catholic Church and characterizes much of the Bible. The Adam and Eve story seems partly a myth about liberation and about every person's attempt to mature to psychological freedom. Eve is to be congratulated rather than blamed, since her disobedience strikes a blow for freedom from patriarchy's repressive power.

Patriarchal societies are characterized by men having authority over women, as in families where males, like Adam, have power over wives and children. Patriarchy is hierarchical, stresses inequality, inclines to intolerance and wishes to dominate. Bishops and priests have traditionally addressed lay Catholics as 'My child', and in recent times the patriarchal power exercised by the Catholic Church has been more paternal; but submission is still expected. History shows that in the past the institutional church has always been ready to resort to coercion and violence when necessary. Patriarchy, as evidenced in the church, is characterized by middle-aged and elderly males exercising authority over youth as well as women, and is threatened by growth in the power of women and the young.

Patriarchy emphasizes duty, what one ought and ought not to do, and praises and blames accordingly. The husband's or father's love has to be earned, can be lost, and can be won again by repenting, obeying and submitting. In patriarchy, love is conditional – conditional on good behaviour, conformity and achievement. In contrast, in matriarchy the mother loves her children not because they do their duty or because of any achievement, but simply because they are her children. In matriarchy, all children are equal in the eyes of the mother, and her love is unconditional. Developmental psychology stresses that such unconditional love is essential for psychological development.

Julian of Norwich sees God's love for us as maternal and unconditional, just there regardless of what we do. The love of Julian's God is not earned by good behaviour, nor lost by sin, and Julian is assured that, regardless of what we do, we never move outside God's protection. She repeatedly declares that God loves us even while we sin. Julian stresses the value of our knowing that God's love and mercy, for ourselves and others, is unconditional and like that of a good mother. The Virgin Mary, as an image of maternal love, is an attempt – history would suggest a largely unsuccessful attempt – to temper the patriarchy of the institutional church.

Belief in male supremacy is central to patriarchy. At the centre of Catholic worship is the mass; only priests can say mass and only men can be priests. In the past, the question of women becoming priests has been considered. But Aquinas, the thirteenth-century theologian, spoke of women's condition of subjection as making them incapable of achieving the eminence of priestly life. Aquinas seemed to regard women as incomplete, as if they were deficient and defective men. So the church justified the exclusion of women from the priesthood, having decided that women were inferior to men on the basis of a primitive account of human nature and biology. Our knowledge of psychology and biology has developed since the Middle Ages, but the exclusion of women from the priesthood and, consequently, from significant power within the church remains. The 1994 papal declaration of John Paul II, in the Apostolic letter *Ordinatio Sacerdotalis*, stated that now, and for all time, women cannot be priests. Thérèse of Lisieux records in her autobiography, *Story of a Soul*, that she felt in herself the vocation to be a priest.

Over the church's long history, women have held positions of power in religious orders and have been superiors in charge of large convents. Occasionally women have been abbesses in charge of monasteries for both men and women; but their authority has usually extended only over women. By the twelfth century, when the power of the papacy over the church was becoming absolute, even this small presence of women in church authority had gone. Among the reasons why the Albigensians and later the Béguines were condemned was because of their positive attitude to women, such as having women preachers. Significantly, until recently, the overwhelming majority of saints canonized by the Roman Catholic Church have been men.

Many Catholics are puzzled and troubled by the church's perception of women and by the subordination of women to men within the church. Christianity affirms full equality of all before God. But historians record that when in the fourth century Christianity became, under Constantine, the official religion of the Roman empire, the church gradually developed into a male-dominated hierarchical institution. Perhaps the psychologist is in a better position than the historian to explain why the Catholic Church has remained so. Social psychologists suggest that organizations which emphasize hierarchical authority are hostile to true equality, such as that between women and men. The authoritarian personality is characterized by a preoccupation with power and control, particularly over people. A patriarchal church manifests obvious power and control in its subordination of women.

And social psychologists have demonstrated that authoritarian traditions dislike change; the Roman Catholic tradition has been and remains essentially authoritarian. Authoritarian personalities have difficulty in coping with the new and in acknowledging the reality of development as an integral part of human existence. The authoritarian tradition regards the nature of things as static. The authoritarian personality regards human nature, particularly, as unchanging and holds that differences between women and men, and differences in their lives, are the result of their different biologies, and so inevitable and permanent. The Catholic Church has not been alone in the past in regarding the purpose of women as family and children. But what modern social psychology reveals, and much of modern secular society now recognizes, is the extent to which human 'nature' is a product of social and cultural factors, and so able to change. In contrast, the Catholic authoritarian tradition fails, or refuses, to recognize the extent to which human beings are shaped by social and cultural factors, and so capable of change.

If the values of women are diffferent from those of men, as Virginia Woolf suggests, and the personalities of women were – and still are – different from those of men, as social psychology suggests, the cause is partly due to the different circumstances of women and men. A liberal tradition recognizes the effect on women, in the past, of having been culturally, socio-economically and power-politically subordinated. A liberal tradition sees that when circumstances change, men and women change too. The church's refusal to abandon an outdated view of women relates partly to the inability of authoritarianism to accept the reality of change. Ordaining women would involve the acceptance of change, which an authoritarian tradition has difficulty in doing.

The subordination of women in the church has also, in the past, been the product of a celibate male priesthood's perception of women as the embodiment of sexuality. This is particularly so in a Catholicism which associates sex with sin. When the celibacy of the clergy was enforced in the twelfth century, celibacy became a rule which eventually became an ideal. The psychological consequence of this was to devalue women and cause them to be seen mainly in terms of their sexuality. Woman came to be regarded in the Catholic Church largely as a sexual and seductive Eve-temptress, and only secondly as a human being.

According to Freudian and object-relations theory accounts, male sexuality suffers from a split. The split causes men to have two images of women – madonna and tart. Men have an idealized romantic fantasy of woman and a contrasting erotic image of woman as sex object. In the New Testament the rift is embodied in the Virgin Mary, the mother of Christ, and Mary Magdalene, the prostitute. Catholicism has elaborated and emphasized these images; Mary is pure madonna, born sinless (the Immaculate Conception), who became the mother of the God-child without having sex (the Virgin Birth), and Mary Magdalene is the sexual fallen woman and prostitute. Such psychological splitting underpins patriarchy.

Psychology recognizes that real and not fantasy women, like real-life men, have within them both dimensions, the feeling-romantic-spiritual and the sexual-erotic-physical. But men's tendency to split women, psychologically, into haloed virgins whom they worship from afar and tart-prostitutes whom they use for their own sexual pleasure, makes it difficult for men to relate to real rather than fantasy women. Object-relations theory sees that the healthy development of male personality involves healing this internal split. Bringing the two images of woman together enables a man to have a proper relationship with a real woman.

In psychoanalytic thought, the split is held to originate in the boy's relationship with mother. The growing boy and adolescent becomes aware that he is forbidden to have sexual feelings about mother. He has to deny any such feelings and hide them even from himself; as a consequence, they become unconscious. The sexless madonna fantasy of women originates in the boy's image of mother, from which he has removed any trace of erotic feeling. Object-relations theory shows how men project this fantasy, with all eroticism removed, on certain other women. The church's celibate male hierarchy, in offering the Virgin Mary as a suitable receptacle for this sexless idealizing projection by men, underpins the split within male personality. The Catholic male is left with his strong erotic feelings and with nowhere to put them; for a time they remain within him in the unconscious. Eventually men tend to project these raw sexual feelings on to certain women and see them as tart, prostitute, whore, temptress, adulteress, witch. Many 'witches' burnt by the church and state, in the late Middle Ages and after, were ordinary women who for varying reasons, sometimes for their challenge to male authority, became targets for men's sexual projection. Significantly, such women were often accused of having sex with the Devil.

Carl Jung recognized that the Catholic tradition of Mary as sinless and sexless made her less human. Catholicism has always had difficulty in positively affirming women's sexuality. And within Catholic patriarchy, Mary who managed motherhood without sex, together with a litany of virgin-saints, has become the object of male madonna fantasies, leaving ordinary women only as embodiments of sexuality. Whatever the value of Catholic teaching on the Virgin, the image of Mary poses problems for both Catholic women and men, making it more difficult for them to acknowledge their own sexuality and shadow. The divided image shores up patriarchy; and Catholicism tends to widen, rather than heal, men's split image of women.

The situation of the celibate Catholic priest is particularly fraught with psychological difficulty. In order for mature sexual love to be possible, a man in a relationship with a woman has to reconcile within himself his images of woman as sexless madonna and prostitute-tart. But the celibate Roman Catholic priest never needs to do so. Catholic priests in their sermons typically idealize Mary, the virgin-mother, and in their personal lives they idealize their own mothers. Young men in Catholic seminaries are likely to adorn their bedrooms walls with photos of their mothers, where other heterosexual males have pictures of wives, girl-friends, fiancées or female pop-stars. The sexual tart-prostitute feelings within celibate priests often remain undealt-with psychologically. This may explain why some Catholic priests, in heterosexual liaisons, seem sometimes to have little interest in real relationships and to take no responsibility for any children that result. The woman was seen only as sexual being; more tender and concerned madonna-wife feelings are reserved for the statue of Mary in the church.

Celibacy is not responsible for the damaging split which psycho-analysis and object relations see as originating in the boy's fantasies about his mother. But a significant sexual relationship with a woman, as in a successful marriage, helps men to bring together the two images of the female. So celibate priests are not well situated to heal the division within them. And men in positions of authority within the church never have close relationships with women who might heal the split since, in patriarchy, women are subordinate and kept psychologically at a distance. Psychology sees that scorn for the feminine and a fear of female sexuality characterize patriarchy.

Patriarchy seems, in personality terms, to be society's embodi-ment of an excessive emphasis on independent stage values and the Jungian animus. As a result, the patriarchal church's view of God is the product of men fixated at the independent stage and dominated by their animus. Such men tend to see God in terms of independ-ence and separateness rather than intimate relationship; of love dependent on good behaviour rather than unconditional love; of power and control rather than caring and compassion; of domin-ation rather than equality. In a patriarchal Catholic Church, there is a tendency for God to remain a remarkably harsh, male and macho God.

The patriarchal nature of the church also emerges in its more recent attitude to homosexuality. Historical records suggest that, for much of earlier Christian history, same-sex relationships were accepted by the church and often blessed and solemnized in religious ceremonies. Boswell's research found throughout Europe manuscripts for same-sex ceremonies, for women as well as men, presided over by priests. But the end of the twelfth century saw the institutional church begin a persecution of those in genital same-sex relationships. Through the thirteenth and fourteenth centuries and later, Western Christendom became obsessively hostile to homo-sexuality.

The late twelfth century saw the arrival of an authoritarian and patriarchal papacy of immense power, which continued unchecked for many centuries. The papacy's achievement of great power is followed by an intensification of the persecution of Jews and heretics and alchemist-scientists, by the late Crusades and the beginning of the Inquisition, by the enforced celibacy of priests, by the end of what little presence women had in the institutional church, by the burning of ordinary women as witches – and by the persecution of gay people.

In the defence mechanism that Freud called 'rationalization', people give lofty but false reasons for what they do, in order to hide their real but less acceptable motives. A father says that he is beating his disobedient son for the boy's own good, but the truth is that really he is enjoying hitting the boy. When we rationalize, in the Freudian sense, we are often unaware of our real motives; the real causes of our actions are unacceptable to ourselves and usually unconscious. The church's objection to women priests can be seen as Freudian rationalization. The church in the past has adduced reasons from biology, and in the present from scripture, as to why women cannot be priests; but psychologists would suggest that the real cause of the church's opposition is the threat which ordained women priests would pose to church patriarchy. Because, in Freudian rationalization, prejudices masquerade as principles and lofty explanations disguise unconscious and base motives, rational-izing usually proves dangerous. Rationalization was behind the papacy's use of the New Testament to justify the church's persecu-tion of Jews. Similarly, the papacy's attempt to condemn homo-sexuality largely on the basis of a few references from scripture seems, to the psychologist, pure Freudian rationalization.

The late medieval papacy and church used the Sodom story in Genesis, and a number of Old Testament verses, as the basis for rationalizing a hostility to homosexuality already existing within the church. The church then went further and used the Sodom story and the Old Testament verses to justify persecuting gay people. But contrary to Old Testament instruction and practice, Catholics happily eat pork, wear clothes made from more than one material, sleep with a menstruating wife, and nowadays Catholics do not kill people committing adultery and do not own slaves. Modern biblical scholarship now sees that what, according to Genesis, happened at Sodom has nothing to do with the ethics of homosexuality; biblical scholars regard the story as clumsily making a statement about hospitality. In spite of this, the 1994 *Catechism of the Catholic Church* still uses the Sodom story to condemn genital gay and lesbian relationships – even though the story presents the gang rape of young women as acceptable! Parts of the Old Testament are, from a Christian perspective, immoral or irrelevant.

It is now the accepted view of the institutional Catholic Church that an informed intelligence has to be applied to understanding all scripture – the New Testament as well as the Old Testament. So the use of a few lines from the New Testament to condemn homosexuality seems further evidence of Freudian rationalization; an authoritarian and patriarchal church's hostility to homosexuality comes first, and finding ways to justify the hostility follows. If we are to take St Paul's ambiguous phrases in the New Testament as condemning homosexuality, then we should also abide by his condemnation of men having long hair, his insistence that women cover their hair and remain silent (in church), and obey their husbands (everywhere), his instruction that since the end is near husbands should live as if they do not have wives, and the emphatic injunction in Acts not to eat blood. We might also conclude that charging interest on money loaned was condemned by scripture, as the church concluded in the past when it condemned usury. The church has also used the anti-Jewish tone of parts of the Gospels to justify its antisemitism. And on the basis of incidents and words in the New Testament (on more than one occasion Paul bids slaves to obey their masters), the church has tolerated slavery. But to these and other examples Catholics now apply common sense – of course, antisemitism and slavery are wrong. Since the church now recognizes the value of an informed intelligence – or an informed common sense – in understanding scripture, the case for condemning homosexuality on the basis of a few ambiguous verses in Paul seems weak. Many people's experience is that they feel sexual love only for those of the same sex, and most psychologists now affirm the goodness of committed same-sex relationships.

According to biblical scholars, St Paul seems to know nothing of those with a gay or lesbian orientation. McNeill, in his study on the Catholic Church and homosexuality, holds that when Paul censures same-sex activity, he is condemning same-sex acts between those who are truly heterosexual, in a context of licentiousness. Paul condemns same-sex acts when this is a deliberate perversion by men and women whose sexuality is really heterosexual, usually associated by Paul with debauchery, prostitution and idol worship. This is light years away from normal loving relationships of gay and lesbian couples. McNeill, an American Jesuit, concludes that Paul's words are not relevant to men and women of a genuinely same-sex orientation.

Modern biblical scholarship reveals that further misinterpretation adds to the confusion surrounding Paul's words. The church has condemned homosexuality as being 'against nature'; but Paul often uses the phrase in a neutral way – as when God acts 'against nature' in grafting the branch (of the Gentiles) on the tree (of the Jews). The church, in attempting to justify its prejudice against same-sex relationships with verses from the Old Testament and Paul, seems guilty of Freudian rationalization. Christ appears to have said nothing about homosexuality.

An unambiguous condemnation of homosexuality cannot be derived from the Bible. There is good evidence that the church accepted same-sex relationships for long periods of earlier Christian history. On the basis of the scientific evidence, modern psychology regards homosexuality and its full genital expression as normal and positive. And most psychologists now recognize that gay and lesbian relationships are as capable of genuine love and commitment as any other kind of human relationship. So what is the real cause of the church's recent hostility to homosexuality? What is hidden behind the church's rationalizing of its current homophobia?

Psychological accounts of personality and of personality development emphasize the importance of relationships for human beings; psychologists regard loving relationships as crucial to establishing our personal identity and our sense of self. Erikson and Jung, for example, regard the right balance of connectedness with others and of independence as essential to human development and achieving personal wholeness. Fairbairn's object-relations theory sees an appropriate relatedness with other people as the primary need of the human person. And most such theories of personality, recognizing our relationship-seeking social being, see our sexuality as expressing a deep need to go out of ourselves to another person. Modern psychology stresses the centrality of relationships in human sexuality.

Even biologically-orientated accounts of personality and development, while acknowledging the place of reproduction, maintain that the function of much human sexual pleasure and practice is primarily psychological, related to bonding. Modern psychologists regard reproduction as only one purpose of human sexual activity and less important than bonding and relationships. Psychologists point out that procreation requires merely a few moments of genital activity, whereas sex is all-pervasive in human life, culture and the arts. With sex so all-pervasive, but so much sexual activity unrelated to procreation, psychological accounts emphasize the crucial role that human sexual activity has in bonding, loving relationships and human identity, all of which fulfil deep human needs and benefit society.

In contrast, the Catholic Church, influenced by the Old Testament, has regarded the purpose of human sexual activity and pleasure as primarily biological, to do with reproduction and child-bearing. Psychology sees the institutional church's condemnation of homosexuality in certain historical periods as connected to the Old Testament tribal directive: Go forth and multiply. Much of the Old Testament is the product of a threatened pastoral society, surrounded by warring tribes, with population growth as an obvious mechanism for survival. The church's past assertion 'Outside the church there is no salvation' is an extreme affirmation of the primacy of the tribe. The Catholic Church's stress on reproduction seems part of a tribal ethic, concerned with survival of the tribe through population growth. The church has implemented this tribal ethic by relating human sexual pleasure – in the past, exclusively – to child-bearing, as evidenced in the ban on artificial methods of birth control.

In view of Christianity's emphasis on love, the modern psychologist regards as ironic the Catholic Church's preoccupation, in human sexuality, with the biological process of reproduction rather than love and relationship. Because of this obsession with reproduction, in the past the church has condemned sexual intercourse between fertile married couples where the intention of procreation was absent. In more recent times, the obsession with reproduction has caused the Catholic Church to condemn, as unnatural or against the 'natural law', sexual activity where procreation is not possible, such as when artifical methods of birth control are used or in homosexuality.

The church in very recent times has qualified the Catholic account of sexuality to give a place to love and bonding. But modern psychology sees the church's continuing emphasis on procreation as evidence of a limited view of personality, which fails to recognize the multi-dimensional nature of the human person. According to psychology, the church still fails to acknowledge adequately the person as a relating being and the extent to which human sexuality expresses the personality's need for a loving relationship. Many psychologists see the church, in still regarding a couple's loving relationship as inseparably linked to the biology of reproduction, as remaining essentially tribal in its view of human sexuality. Psychologists, while recognizing the importance of biology, see the human person as social through and through and more than just biology. Psychology reveals unambiguously the multi-dimensional nature of human beings and the independent place of love, relationship and bonding in human sexuality.

Modern psychology's emphasis on human bonding, love and relationships as a central and independent function of sexual activity and pleasure undermines the church's present hostility to homosexuality. If what constitutes the basis for heterosexual marriage is a loving relationship, and not reproduction, then loving same-sex relationships are equally valid. Psychology sees gay and lesbian relationships as valid because human sexual activity is really about relationships of love between two people, far more than about procreation. According to psychology, the church's present hostility to homosexuality is partly a return to an Old Testament tribal culture, where morality relates psychologically to reproduction and the survival of the tribe. It is difficult to know whether this element of church tribal culture is an atavistic return to an Old Testament ethic or an unconscious belief that emphasizing the importance of child-bearing helps the church to grow. But in such a culture, homosexuality comes to be regarded as dangerous, a form of non-conformity threatening society by its inability to produce the children required for the tribe's survival and growth.

But hostility to homosexuality can also result when any non-conformity or divergence from the norm is regarded by people, especially those with power, as a threat to society. So liberal societies, generally more tolerant of non-conformity, are more tolerant of homosexuality than authoritarian societies. In Adorno's *The Authoritarian Personality* study, authoritarian personalities expressed, as well as antisemitism and racism, hostility to homo-sexuality. *The Authoritarian Personality* revealed that the under-lying strand, unifying the seemingly disparate targets of the authoritarian personality's hostility, was an acceptance only of people like themselves. Authoritarian personalities and traditions are intolerant of difference and hostile to people whom they see as different from themselves, such as gay men and lesbians. An authoritarian church in medieval Christian Europe persecuted Jews who were non-conformist simply as a result of holding to their Jewish faith. An authoritarian church has persecuted others not conforming such as heretics, non-believers, alchemist-scientists and those in different Christian traditions. With gay men and lesbians, that the difference relates to sexuality is relevant; *The Authoritarian Personality* research showed authoritarian person-alities to be obsessively concerned with sex, which they associate with sin and guilt. In contrast to the church's intolerance of homo-sexuality, which an authoritarian church sees as divergent non-conformity, modern psychology emphasizes the normality of same-sex relationships.

The Catholic Church is also hostile to homosexuality because of the nature of the church's patriarchy. In the Sodom story in Genesis, Lot invites the men of the town to make sexual use of his daughters. The Bible is suggesting that to meet the obligations of hospitality, by preventing his male guests from being sexually assaulted, Lot should let his two daughters be gang-raped. But the principles of patriarchy, and its sexual rules in particular, invariably have a hidden agenda, which is to state that only what men do is important, and to assert that women are inferior and exist largely for men's use. Patriarchy is often hostile to homosexuality because, in the sexuality of gay men, a man adopts the role of a woman, which patriarchal societies frequently view as demeaning the status of the male. In the patriarchal perspective of the Catholic Church, men must not lower themselves to the status of women by taking a woman's sexual position. As the Catholic Church became more patriarchal, the church became hostile to homosexuality and the persecution of gay people began.

The church takes its cue from the Old Testament, which begins with the Adam and Eve story and makes clear that the male is in charge. For a man to adopt the woman's role in intercourse is, in the agenda of a patriarchal Catholic Church, to identify in a disturbing and demeaning way with woman's inferior and subordinate position. A patriarchal church probably finds lesbianism also unacceptable for a similar reason; patriarchy holds that women who in a lesbian relationship adopt a more assertive role are usurping the role which patriarchy regards as the prerogative of the male. But the relevant verses in the Bible appear to show less concern with lesbianism, possibly because sexual relationships between women appear less of a threat to patriarchy than relationships between men. Patriarchy's rules about sex, written by men, are to create and maintain a social order in which women are inferior to men and where only what men do is important. And since Catholic patriarchy regards a man in a gay relationship as demeaning the status of the male by seemingly acting the part of a woman, and since in a lesbian relationship a woman may adopt a role which Catholic patriarchy regards as a male preserve, homosexuality also challenges the attitude to women that characterizes a patriarchal church. The subordination of women and hostility to homosexuality are related in a patriarchal Catholic Church.

Tribalism, authoritarianism and a patriarchal agenda co-exist within the institutional church. An explanation in terms of

Freudian rationalization reveals that among the real causes of the church's hostility to same-sex relationships is a tribal concern for the reproduction of offspring, an authoritarian preoccupation with conformity to a sexual norm and a patriarchal assertion of male dominance. A church that is less tribal, and not obsessed with procreation, would place greater emphasis on love and relationships in human sexuality. A church that is less authoritarian, and not obsessed with power and conformity, would find departures from the norm acceptable and welcome difference. A church that is less patriarchal, and not obsessed with male domination, would begin truly asserting the equality of women and enable women to take their rightful place in the church. A less tribal, authoritarian and patriarchal Catholic Church would affirm the goodness and holiness of same-sex relationships as an expression of committed human love.

The present institutional church is intolerant of non-conformity, bans artificial methods of birth control, condemns the sexuality of gay men and lesbians, insists on a celibate priesthood and subordinates women. In contrast with Christianity's central image, of a man not as powerful oppressor but as crucified and powerless victim, there persists beneath the veneer of the institutional church a harsh, authoritarian and patriarchal God who loves only conditionally and is male. When in 1950 the Catholic Church declared infallible the dogma of the Assumption, the belief that Mary had been taken bodily into heaven, Carl Jung was pleased. Jung, stressing that he was not questioning any metaphysical reality expressed by the teaching, valued the dogma as a symbolic expression of the feminine being incorporated into the Godhead. The dogma of the Assumption can be seen, psychologically, as an attempt by the Catholic Church to bring more of the feminine into a male and patriarchal Christian God. Jung, on the basis of his considerable anthropological knowledge, reports in *Answer to Job* that 'it was recognized even in prehistoric times that the primordial divine being is both male and female'.

7

The Institutional Church

What frightens me is the Church as a social structure. Not only on account of its blemishes, but from the very fact that it is something social.

(Simone Weil, *Waiting on God*)

Certainly, if I am obliged to bring religion into after-dinner toasts (which indeed does not seem quite the thing), I shall drink – to the Pope, if you please, – still, to conscience first, and to the Pope afterwards.

(Cardinal Newman, *Letter to the Duke of Norfolk*)

The Sabbath was made for human beings; human beings were not made for the Sabbath.

(St Mark's Gospel 2.27)

In the text of the *Republic*, Plato speaks of the Great Beast; Simone Weil sees the Great Beast as a metaphor for society and its human institutions. For Simone, to conform totally to the values and prejudices of society and its institutions is to serve the Great Beast. She held that thinking and acting in complete conformity to the Great Beast, such as by submitting unreservedly to the church, impairs the individual's search for God.

Simone loved the Gospels, the church's ceremonies and prayers, the living tradition of a human community seeking God. She was aware that the church needed an institutional structure in order to continue existing; but she was appalled by the Catholic Church's long record of intolerance and persecution of others. Though the Catholic Church does appear to have a particularly scandalous history, especially from the late twelfth century, Simone Weil detected something inherently dangerous in the power that all social institutions have over us. Why, she asks, did seemingly good and holy men, among them saints, approve of the Crusades and the

Inquisition? Her answer is that they they were blinded by the social institution of the church. Simone does not distrust community but only the power of the Great Beast.

Simone valued the contribution of the church to the spiritual lives of individuals; but social psychology confirms that she was right in emphasizing the dangers of the institutional church. Psychological research demonstrates that prejudice and intolerance are often the product of conformity to institutions. Even seemingly liberal Catholics have persecuted and done violence to others in obedience to the church. Research reveals the intense pressure on individuals in organizations to obey orders, regardless of the contents of those orders. Milgram's research demonstrates the danger of individuals becoming mere agents of higher authorities, particularly in hierarchical organizations like the church. Milgram's studies show that people subordinate in situations of hierarchical authority, regarding themselves as agents of others, often cease to be responsible moral individuals and obey orders which would seem morally wrong. Simone too recognized that what often concerns those in organizations is not an order's content but carrying out the order correctly. In *Gravity and Grace* she declares, referring to the Great Beast of society: 'Nothing seems evil to those who serve it except failure in its service.'[1] History records evils done by ordinary Catholics in obedience to the orders of popes, bishops and other religious superiors.

So psychology would seem to confirm that Simone was right in believing that what caused good men, and some saints, to support evils such as the Crusades and the Inquisition was the social pressure of the institutional church. Psychology recognizes how difficult it is for members of an organization to disobey. Social psychology has demonstrated time and again how group norms influence our thought and behaviour. People think and act in certain ways often merely because of the pressures in an organization to conform. Throughout many centuries, often ordinary Roman Catholics have persecuted Jews largely in conformity to the anti-semitism of the papacy and the institutional church. At certain periods of history, ordinary Catholics have persecuted heretics, gay people, reformers, non-believers, non-Catholic Christians and others, again in obedience to popes and institutional church. In *Gravity and Grace* Simone says: 'Conscience is deceived by the social.'[2] She calls attention to the terrifying power that institutions, such as the church, have over the thoughts, beliefs and actions of those of us who belong to them.

Simone Weil saw that the power of a social organization results partly from members experiencing the institution as having a certain transcendence. There is always a danger, she believed, that members come to regard the institution as an end in itself, with its existence unrelated to the needs of individuals and the wider society. Psychology, too, recognizes the tendency for an institution's primary goals, such as preaching God's kingdom, to become secondary to the institution's survival. The social misleads us into regarding an organization, such as 'the church', as of absolute value and worthy of our unconditional love, obedience and service. Psychology sees that dangerous consequences are likely when an institution's reputation, survival and growth become the primary goal of the organization, and when the needs of the individual and wider society become secondary. In the past, Catholic authorities, dealing with abuse of children by priests, have often seemed more concerned about the church's reputation than with the welfare of the abused children and with protecting other children; until recently, Catholic authorities have often attempted to avoid any scandal by concealing the matter and not informing police and other statutory authorities.

Uncritical service of the Great Beast is part of the authoritarian tradition; an authoritarian hierarchy has regarded the institutional church as God's kingdom on earth. Simone saw that service of the institutional church has often become, in Catholicism, a substitute for a relationship with God and serving our neighbour. But Simone regarded individuals as more important than institutions and believed that no institution, not even the church, should be the object of our unqualified love and loyalty. In the Catholic liberal tradition, individuals and not institutions are ends in themselves, and the institutional church exists to bring about God's kingdom through serving individual human beings.

Simone maintained that excessive conformity to the institutional church placed at risk our search for truth. In her view, the Catholic Church had during its history often threatened, and even suppressed, the free intellectual enquiry which she believed to be essential in the search for God; the church's past animosity to science was only one example of its hostility to intellectual freedom. And the church's antagonism to science originated not from ordinary Catholics, many of whom made significant contributions to scientific knowledge, but from the institutional church.

Simone saw the church as maintaining that God has no obligations but only rights in regard to human beings; she saw the institutional church then claiming that such a view of God gave to the church the right of absolute control over people's minds. Simone held that as a result of such an authoritarian claim the church based its teaching not on rational discussion and evidence, but on its own self-justifying authority. The church then attempted to force its members to think and feel according to the church's dictates. Simone comments in *Waiting on God*: 'This abuse of power is not of God. It comes from the natural tendency of every form of collectivism, without exception, to abuse power.'[3] She felt that the Catholic Church's emphasis on authority and obedience made it almost impossible for those who were Catholic – and for her, if she were to become one – to remain intellectually honest.

Simone Weil recognized that the church's authoritarianism had often impeded, or blocked, the development of valuable insights and of new ways for expressing religious truths. Such developments have usually been initiated by individuals outside the church's hierarchical structure; and they have often been implemented by individuals in spite of resistance from the institutional church. Simone argued that, in the search for God and truth, the individual human intelligence requires the freedom which in the past has been denied by the church.

But Simone did not advocate total freedom for the individual intelligence; she saw dangers in the excessive individualism of unqualified freedom. And though aware that the church had often been wrong in the past, she declared that the church might sometimes need to restrain individuals when they argued for action of which the institutional church disapproved. Even when the explorations of individuals remained in the realm of the theoretical and abstract, Simone felt the church would be justified in warning Catholics about such thought, but never in attempting to stifle their thought. She recognized that the different perspectives of individual and institution made difficult balancing the claims of the individual Catholic and the institutional church. Acceding to the demands of the individual too generously leads to excessive libertarianism, and yielding too much to the claims of the institution results in totalitarianism. But observing the Roman Catholic Church in history and in her own time, she had no doubts that the church was guilty of the second.

Simone believed that all of us have the potential to liberate ourselves from a constricting subordination to the Great Beast. Simply examining and becoming aware of the dangers is a beginning: 'To contemplate the social,' says Simone in *Gravity and Grace*, 'is as good a way of detachment as to retire from the world.'⁴ A first and effective step is, for the Catholic, both to realize how often the institutional church has been wrong and to acknowledge the evils of which the church has been guilty.

Among other features of the institutional Catholic Church that Simone particularly disliked was the church's past refusal to recognize the presence and the workings of God in other religions and beliefs. She also deplored the failure of the church to acknowledge God's presence even among atheists; she stressed the importance of recognizing in the sufferings of atheists and agnostics an implicit acceptance of God's will. Simone saw that a church can be parochial even when its members number hundreds of millions, and she disliked what she regarded as a sort of Catholic patriotism, manifested in an excessive allegiance to the church; she felt that a Christian's love should be directed equally to the whole world.

Centuries before Simone Weil, Julian had remarked that in contrast to a caring and compassionate God, the church seemed more concerned with judgment. Since God and Christ had always appeared in Julian's revelations as a mother who loved unconditionally, Julian was troubled by this judging church. She concluded that the church needed to be judging, even when God is so loving, because the church has to guide us on earth; but Julian appears unconvinced by her own explanation. Simone's explanation would be that the church is an institution – and God is not! But Simone also maintained that much of what she disliked about the Catholic Church originated not just from its being an institution but, specifically, from its being an organization with particular values.

Social psychology demonstrates that the values of an organization have important consequences. Psychology would attribute much of Catholicism's intolerance and persecution of others to the values of the institutional church, and to a church structure embodying, reinforcing and even forming those values. The dangers of institutions are greatly augmented in Catholicism by the institutional church's claim to exclusive divine authority, by a valuing of the organization above individual members, by an excessive allegiance to the institutional church, and by an authoritarian and patriarchal tradition. These values are embodied in the structure of an exclusively male hierarchy, and in a centralized power structure of a papacy claiming infallibility and of institutions surrounding the papacy, such as the Roman Curia.

When an organization's structure is hierarchical, and when people in the hierarchy prize their own authority and are accountable to no one, the more likely they are to be corrupted by power and the greater their corruption is likely to be. And in a hierarchical structure where those with power regard obedience to their authority as a central value, the less do those in subordinate positions hold themselves responsible for their own actions in obedience to that authority. Milgram speaks of conscience being 'diminished at the point of entering a hierarchical structure' (*Obedience to Authority*). Pressure to conform and obey, powerful in a secular organization, is even stronger in an authoritarian and hierarchical church claiming divine authority.

Catherine of Siena is indicative. Her report in the *Dialogue*, of God warning that anyone disobeying the pope is in danger of damnation, illustrates Catherine conforming to the institutional church. In an authoritarian church, non-conformity is seen as an especially serious sin; and in the later Middle Ages, disobedience to the pope was regarded as heresy for which people were burnt at the stake. That Catherine, who spent years lovingly working among the destitute and tending the sick during plague, should at times see God as so harsh, confirms psychology's view that authoritarian and hierarchical institutions psychologically harm individuals. When the views of Catherine and her God are judgmental and damning, they seem simply those of a Catholic conforming to an oppressive and authoritarian fourteenth-century papacy. Catherine, being true to herself, gives a different message. Addressing God in the *Dialogue* she says: 'No matter where I turn, I find nothing but your deep burning charity.'[5]

The values of the four women and their God largely express what modern philosophers have termed an ethic of care. In this caring ethic, love and compassion and care come before all else. People who adopt a caring ethic hold that what really matters is responding to the needs of others; they regard caring for the individual in a network of relationships as morally more important than obedience to rules. 'I understood that LOVE COMPRISED ALL VOCATIONS,' writes Thérèse in *Story of a Soul*, 'THAT LOVE WAS EVERYTHING, THAT IT EMBRACED ALL TIMES AND PLACES.'[6]

What matters in an ethic of care is that no one should be left out; a caring ethic often has reservations about particular rules and principles because they exclude. The rule that marriage is for life excludes those whose marriages fail. And nothing could be more excluding than the Catholic Church's past principle of 'No salvation outside the church'. An ethic of care holds that all people should be included and that everyone has an equal right to love, compassion and happiness, not just those who obey the rules. But though in a caring ethic, love and compassion do not have to be won or earned, the ethic of care still holds that principles relating to right and wrong exist. And an ethic of care recognizes that it is generally possible to decide what is right and wrong. But the caring ethic also sees that rules and principles about right and wrong are often man-made and made by men with power, such as popes. As a consequence, an ethic of care is not only reluctant to judge others but often questions the rules and principles by which people are judged. What matters to those motivated by an ethic of care is individuals and relationships; and they give reasons for what they do in terms of other people's needs. Julian's *Revelations of Divine Love* expresses an ethic of care.

Simone Weil had realized that institutions have difficulty with caring and compassion for individuals. Institutions tend to adopt what philosophers have termed an ethic of justice, which philosophers regard as largely having dominated moral thinking in Western society. A true ethic of justice asserts valuable universal principles, such as the equality of all human beings. An ethic of justice regards moral behaviour in terms of general rules which are claimed as applicable to all, such as 'marriage is a permanent relationship'. An ethic of justice, having formulated abstract principles and general rules, emphasizes that individuals are to be judged and punished according to whether they obey or disobey these principles and rules. Even in the New Testament, the rich man in hell who asks for pity is told by Abraham that he has squandered his chance and now there can be no mercy for him. Those who adopt an ethic of justice contend that, from a ranking of principles and rules, they can reason logically to definitive judgments on every act of every human being.

Institutions do not inevitably adopt an ethic of justice, but size will incline them to do so. In a large organization, rules and regulations are usually emphasized; relationships tend towards the functional, involve little feeling and are likely to be formal rather than personal. In theory, the Catholic Church has adopted a justice ethic, with principles and rules such as – all human beings are equal in the eyes of God, everyone should respect their parents, artificial methods of birth control are wrong, we should care for the sick, Catholics must obey the pope. In practice, the Catholic Church seems often to have operated in terms of a debased justice ethic.

Whatever the value of an ethic of justice, based as it is on principles, history provides an unending record of physical and psychological violence done by human beings to other human beings in the name of some principle. The institutional church has murdered Jews, persecuted non-Catholic Christians and pagans and gay people, slaughtered heretics, burned ordinary women as supposed witches, executed alchemist-scientists and been responsible for blood-stained Crusades and Inquisitions. And the insti-

tutional church has justified this violence done to others on the basis
of principles such as the defence of the church, of Christian society
and of Catholic morals. The violence and evil done in the name of
supposed principles would seem a radical limitation of a justice
ethic.

And many principles once used by the institutional church to
justify its violence and persecution of others are no longer held by
the church; this suggests another limitation to the church's application of a justice ethic. If Catholicism's rules and principles are
occasionally altered and sometimes come to be regarded as wrong,
how can they be – as the church claims – definitive, unchanging and
God-given? The persecution of others has been justified by the
church on the basis of principles such as 'Error has no rights' and
the primacy of 'Catholic truth' over personal conscience and belief.
But during the Second Vatican Council the church acknowledged
the rights of conscience and conceded a certain freedom to personal
belief. Similarly, the church, with the dogma of 'Outside the
church there is no salvation', justified the violent conversion of non-
believers on the principle of saving their souls. But the church now
regards such past violence as wrong. And the church has ceased to
hold that there is no salvation outside the church.

The institutional church no longer condemns charging interest
on money loaned as, in principle, immoral. The papacy no longer
condemns, on the principle that hierarchy and inequality are of
divine origin, attempts to achieve a more egalitarian secular society.
In the nineteenth century, in the name of principle, the institutional church condemned democracy and human rights; a century
later these are now approved by the church, again in the name of
principle. Changes over time of rules and principles, claimed by the
church as God-given, reveal them often to be mere constructions of
church authority. The caution implicit in an ethic of care, with
regard to church rules and principles, would appear to be justified.
And within Catholicism, there has been a constant tendency for the
institutional church's ethic of justice to become debased.

The church's past and present condemnations, in the name of
supposed principles, are often the product of Freudian rationalization; an ethic of justice appears particularly vulnerable to

Freudian rationalizing, where we hide our real and unacceptable motives behind a show of impressively elevated principles. Frequently an ethic of justice becomes debased; and bigotry disguised by rationalization persecutes people and condemns beliefs in the name of supposed principles. Significantly, the church, with prejudices masquerading as principles, has been particularly prone to condemn and persecute when the papacy and the institutional church has been at its most powerful.

In contrast to the church's violent application of a justice ethic, an ethic of care holds that no rule or principle exists for which another's life should be sacrificed. An ethic of care regards individual people as always prior to principles. And though the Catholic Church no longer attempts to justify its history of violence done to others, the institutional church often appears still to regard a justice ethic's rules and principles as more important than the caring ethic's love and compassion for people.

Another limitation of a justice ethic, related to its exclusion of others on the basis of rules and principles, is self-righteousness among those regarding themselves as included and on the inside. The included tend to feel superior to those outside the charmed circle, which explains the superior moral tone of many church pronouncements. The justice ethic's emphasis on exclusion also explains the contrast between the benevolence of popes and Roman Curia to conforming members of the church, and their hostility to independent priests and bishops who criticize the church or them.

The Catholic Church has been controlled by males and, historically, the justice ethic has been more characteristic of men than women. It seems likely that men have recourse to the ethic of justice often because they have difficulty with caring relationships. Confronted by a human problem, men are inclined to resort to abstract principles rather than solve a specific situation with a caring ethic's love and compassion. The parish priest, faced with a situation that could be solved or alleviated by genuine caring, might turn to the *Catechism of the Catholic Church* and just follow church rules.

A further limitation of the justice ethic is that rules and principles are not as all-encompassing as might be supposed. When general principles clash, there is often no higher principle or rule to resolve the conflict. Individuals motivated by the justice ethic are often forced to make a difficult choice about which principle to follow. In contrast, an ethic of care proposes a universality of love, care and compassion. And the caring ethic's abiding assertion, that everyone has a right to a relationship in which they are cared for, implies the principle of human equality which a modern justice ethic stresses. In the Gospel, the Good Samaritan extends the caring ethic's compassion and concern for those he knows to those he does not know. For Simone Weil, justice is the general principle that loving one's neighbour takes in responding to the needs of people unknown to us. Simone holds that in following Christ's command to love our neighbour as ourself we are meeting the abstract claims of justice for others: 'The Gospel makes no distinction between the love of our neighbour and justice' (*Waiting on God*).[7] In this way, an ethic of care generalizes and becomes the universal principle that we should be caring and compassionate in our relationships with everyone.

The suggestion that caring values originate in situations of intimate and informal relationships, such as family, might explain why women, usually more involved in the family, tend to adopt a caring ethic. Women do not differ from men in the intellectual processes involved in an ethic of justice, such as the capacities to handle abstract thought, to rank general principles in an ordered structure and to deduce logically to conclusions. But moral philosophers have noted that women regard these cerebral processes as peripheral when it comes to human relationships. Philosophers point out that abstract and general principles are not central to the way most women relate to their children.

Some feminists see a danger in relating the caring dimension especially to women; they stress that caring for others has been the reality of women's lives down the ages. Such feminists regard woman's care and compassion for others, however valuable, as partly a product of women's subordination to men; they argue that believing caring values to be related particularly to women serves to maintain their subordination. Other feminists see as central to the emergence of an ethic of care women's involvement in the life processes of birth, nurturing and raising children, to which men by and large have remained peripheral. These feminists suggest that, as a result of women's involvement in such basic life processes over the ages, women's more caring way of thinking is quite simply morally superior to men's and certainly more human. They argue that women's superior ethic of care should by and large replace the male ethic of justice, pointing to the Abraham and Isaac story to illustrate the inadequacies of a justice ethic.

Abraham is ready, however reluctantly, to sacrifice his son, presumably in conformity to the general principle that God should be obeyed. A mother, motivated by caring values, might be less willing to put her child's life at risk for so general and abstract a notion. The Old Testament God is operating here in terms of a justice ethic. *He* is prepared to give the impression of threatening Isaac's life, and to risk damaging the child's relationship with his father, in order to test Abraham and make the point that he really does not want such sacrifices. This God seems more concerned with establishing a general principle than caring for a specific child and a specific father. A more female God, certainly a God more guided by an ethic of care, would have found a more compassionate way of making the point.

It seems likely that ethics of care and justice operating at the social level connect at the level of personality to anima and animus, and to the relating and independent stages. And though men also have a deep need for ethic of care values, usually less obviously than women, a male hierarchy within the church has constantly emphasized the justice ethic. The institutional church's imbalanced preoccupation with a justice ethic needs to be redressed.

The thoughts of our four women suggest a need for the church to adopt more of an ethic of care, even at times to substitute a caring ethic for the justice ethic which has usually characterized the church. And for much of history, the institutional church has operated largely in terms of a debased ethic of justice. The Catholic Church has both inclined to a debased justice ethic, and been particularly vulnerable to all the dangers of a justice ethic, because church values and structure have been hierarchical, authoritarian and patriarchal. A hierarchical church has been more preoccupied with its own authority than with genuine caring for the individual.

An authoritarian church, unaware of its fallibility, has refused to consider that its rules and principles might be wrong. A male patriarchal church, ill at ease with a caring ethic's love and compassion, has been always ready to resort to coercion and violence.

A church characterized by a caring ethic would be more concerned with care and compassion for people than with enforcing its own rules. And Simone Weil believed that the church would be of more value, and the power of the Great Beast reduced within the church, when the primary concern of the institutional church became individual people and not its own survival. Even in recent times, when a priest's sexual relations with a woman have become known, Catholic hierarchies, in an inversion of caring ethic values, have often been concerned more with protecting the church's reputation than with the well-being of individuals involved, such as the woman, any children and the priest. For Simone, the essential purpose of the church is to help individuals grow to God, by providing an environment which fosters psychological and spiritual development. In Simone's view, the individual's growth to God is more likely to be nurtured by an institutional church which regards its obligations to individuals as prior to any rights over them.

Simone argued that within an institution relationships need to be based on a sense of obligation; one of the pope's titles is 'servant of the servants of God'. She held that fulfilling our obligation to others, through caring for them as individuals, should become a basis both for the institutional church and for our own personal morality. Such a caring for others, emerging from a sense of obligation, is a central element in an ethic of care. Simone maintained that if relationships within the church were based on a sense of obligation to others, the institutional church would become more of a bridge between human beings and God. For Simone, how the church should regard its individual members, and how each of us should regard each other, emanates from the recognition of something sacred in every human individual.

Simone is aware that some needs can only be met through society and community. She recognizes that whatever the dangers and limitations of the social, we cannot manage without society and its institutions. But Simone holds that any respect due to a collectivity, such as family or church, is not on account of anything relating to the institution itself but because of what that institution gives to people. She held that institutions like the church should be respected to the extent that they give meaning and worth to individual human lives.

But even if the church were to replace, with an enlightened ethic of justice, the debased justice ethic characterizing the institutional church through much of history, this would still prove inadequate; the justice ethic has many limitations. The relation between an ethic of care and an enlightened ethic of justice needs to be constantly negotiated within an organization; but for centuries the institutional church has emphasized an extreme justice ethic. And an ethic of care's emphasis on the unique individual, on each individual's unique situation, on concern and compassion for others, on relationships, has often been devalued by the institutional church. For Catholicism to become both fully human and Christian, the institutional church needs to redress the imbalance of centuries either by replacing its largely debased ethic of justice with an ethic of care or, at the very least, by adopting both a caring ethic and an enlightened justice ethic.

The church also needs to move from a preoccupation with the institution of the church to a greater concern for individual people and their experience. The New Testament continually stresses the caring ethic of love, relationships and compassion; for Christ, the unique individual comes first. Christ's words in the Gospel, 'The Sabbath was made for human beings; human beings were not made for the Sabbath', express a caring ethic's concern for individuals before rules and principles.

Thérèse of Lisieux also stresses the importance of individual people. In the many biographies written of Thérèse, she is portrayed as a dutiful daughter of the church; and her biographers often emphasize a preoccupation with obedience and submissiveness to convent rules. But a deeper analysis reveals in Thérèse's life a subversive element of protest against the constraints of institutions. It would seem that, for Thérèse, the individual is more important than the rules of convent, religious order and church.

Thérèse values the guidance and support of the church. But she expresses an awareness that if all judgment is left to the church and we preoccupy ourselves with church rules and how best to obey them, we remain immature. Time and again what becomes apparent in Thérèse's own life is the significance of her own experience. She never doubts the church's importance for her; but she finds equally valuable, at times more valuable, her own religious insight, her own experience of God and her feeling of being accepted and loved by God. Such experience takes on a particular importance for Thérèse in times of uncertainty, when any answer to be found is to be found within herself.

She also stresses the uniqueness of the individual and the individual's experience. Thérèse's appreciation of human differences emerges when she says in *Story of a Soul*, 'I understand, however, that all souls cannot be the same.'[8] Thérèse's God is a mother who – in an ethic of care way – regards all her differing children with equal caring and compassion. Thérèse stresses the value to God of ordinary people and of ordinary people's experience, and she sees ordinary people 'empowered' by a knowledge of God within them and by the experience of the Divine.

Centuries before Thérèse, Julian also had seen God as a mother who regards all her children as equally valuable. Julian's God is a mother who remains always close, loves each of us unconditionally and would not think of judging or punishing her children. 'But I could not see anger or blame in God,'[9] Julian reports in the *Revelations*. She regards God as a mother who lovingly enfolds all human beings in a network of relationships.

With occasional exceptions in Catherine's *Dialogue*, the God portrayed by the four women is characterized by an ethic of care. Their God is more interested in relationships than in rules, in compassion and concern for the needs of all rather than with judgment. Their God, recognizing the uniqueness of every individual and of every individual's experience, embraces all in a motherly love which does not have to be earned. And the four women believe that God is caring, loving and compassionate simply because it is God's nature to be caring, loving and compassionate. In order to reflect this caring God, the church needs to replace a justice ethic's emphasis on rules, obedience to rules and judging people in terms of rules, with a caring ethic emphasis on love and compassion for all. God's instruction to Catherine, 'Give up judgment,'[10] would seem to apply to the institutional church as much as to the rest of us.

But in spite of a caring ethic appearing to express God's unconditional love in a way that the justice ethic often fails to, the church has usually been dominated in the past and remains dominated in the present by an ethic of justice, and often by a debased justice ethic. The church's insistence on the primacy of rules and principles, supposedly absolute but which change, has made people less important than principles. Faced with marriage breakdown, the church now often annuls a marriage on the grounds that a marriage relationship never existed; such a strategy saves the principle of the permanence of marriage but ignores any hurt that denying a relationship ever existed might do to the couple or their children. Such an approach is typical of the justice ethic.

An ethic of care sees rules painted not in strong primary colours but in shades of grey. A caring ethic undoubtedly asserts the moral good of the permanence of marriage but recognizes that sometimes there are situations where it might be right to invoke a lesser good. Avoiding damage to both partners and the children, and bringing God's love to those involved, might require the lesser good of accepting the reality of the breakdown of a true marriage, making an exception to the rule of permanence and annulling the marriage. A Catholic hierarchy operating in terms of an ethic of care would understand that the couple once had loved, had a relationship and been truly married, but the relationship and marriage have now ended. The caring ethic recognizes the limits of many supposedly absolute rules. For a caring ethic, many such rules are not absolute but compassion is.

The church, in its preoccupation with rules and principles, often negates both caring and justice. A Catholic marries in a registry office or simply cohabits, while another marries in a church. If the relationships of both break down, the first is able to marry in a Catholic Church, but any second relationship the other enters into is regarded by the church as adultery. A Catholicism characterized by a caring ethic would recognize that many rules and principles, claimed as God-given by the church, were often made by men. The caring ethic sees the institutional church's emphasis on rules as always threatening an absolute law of love and compassion. 'I understand so well,' says Thérèse in *Story of a Soul*, 'that it is only love that makes us acceptable to God.'[11]

The caring ethic values human experience. In accordance with the Catholic liberal tradition, an ethic of care stresses the relevance, in formulating rules and principles, of human experience and the reality of human nature as it is. And a caring ethic, partly as a result of its origins in the family and other face-to-face relationships, prompts us to put the good of individual people before general rules and abstract principles. Parish priests, daily experiencing in their work the suffering of specific human beings, are tending more to ignore the inflexible rules dictated by a distant Curia in favour of an ethic of care's compassion. In contrast, the canon lawyers of Rome, remote from other people's pain and seemingly unaware of the varying realities of different human lives, seem more concerned with abstractions relating to a non-existent world. But an ethic of care holds that morality must take into account, even make its starting point, human experience and the diversity of human psychology. A more Christ-like church would be guided less by the abstract principles of a justice ethic historically characteristic of men. An increased concern for the individual and a move to an ethic of care, both characteristic of Christ and historically associated with women, would modify church values and change church structure.

Women will undoubtedly become a powerful force for change within the church. But evidence would seem to suggest that male values only cease to dominate an institution when women occupy a significant number of influential positions within the organization, such as a third. And it is possible that values associated with women, which the church appears particularly to need, will make it difficult for women to rise to positions of influence within the church. There is evidence that even in commercial organizations women's motivation differs from that of men; women tend to be more motivated by the intrinsic satisfaction of doing their work well than are men, who usually seek external rewards such as promotion. If the overall values and structure of the church fail to change, then men, more concerned with promotion, and more competitive and confrontational than women, will retain the significant positions of influence within the institutional church. In a Catholic Church whose values and structure remain for the present authoritarian, patriarchal and excessively hierarchical, women with a caring ethic's sensitivity to the feelings of others are unlikely to rise to positions of influence. Such women would be too Christian for promotion within the Catholic Church!

Significantly, the changes in values that feminist psychologists regard as necessary within secular organizations to enable women progress are mostly in the direction of caring ethic values. Feminist organization psychologists report that women are happier in organizations which are more concerned with relationships, where there is more sensitivity to our need for relating to others, and which place greater emphasis on communication and connectedness with others. Feminist philosophers maintain that women prefer organizations where there is a place for feelings and co-operation, and where there exists greater concern for individual people than for the organization. Feminist psychologists hold that women prefer organizations where equality is valued.

But feminists, in relation to commercial situations, have stressed the danger of values and structures of organizations remaining the same – and the women in the organizations changing. Similarly, social psychology's recognition of the power of organizations makes us aware that what might change is not the church but women in the church: women might be socialized into the male values and structures which still dominate the institutional church. For this reason, an understanding of the underlying psychological processes involved is important. For example, as a result of social pressure, women holding positions in the church might change to being more concerned for the needs of the institutional church than for those of individual members. Similarly, women in the institutional church might conform and, acquiescing in the ethos of extreme hierarchy, seek promotion within that hierarchy, rather than question the presence of extreme hierarchical structure within the church. Within a male church ethos, women might eventually become excessively influenced by an ethic of justice, even by a debased ethic of justice.

And there are likely to be many men in the church hierarchy reluctant to accept changes that involve relinquishing elements of a justice ethic or abandoning the debased justice ethic which, for so long, has characterized the institutional church. In contrast, many men in secular society, Roman Catholics among them, are becoming more motivated in their personal and work lives by ethic of care values. It seems also true that more priests, faced by suffering people whose problems can be solved or alleviated by love and compassion and by less emphasis on church rules, wish to move towards the values associated with a caring ethic.

Social psychology confirms that Simone Weil was right in stressing the dangers of institutions. A central feature of Catholic history is the institutional church's intolerance and violence done to others. But social psychology demonstrates that certain organizational values and structures add to the dangers of institutions. And in the Catholic Church the dangers common to many institutions have been augmented by certain organizational values: excessive emphasis on a justice ethic – even on a debased justice ethic, inordinate loyalty to the church, belief in the church's rules as God-given and never defective or erroneous, authoritarianism, patriarchy and subordination of the individual to the supposed good of the organization. Related to these values are structural elements of the church, such as extreme hierarchy and excessive centralization of power in institutions such as the papacy and Curia. Though the church has changed, many of these values and much of this structure, together responsible for past intolerance and violence done to others, remain largely unchanged in the contemporary institutional church. Since the church retains in its values and structure much from the past, such as authoritarianism, patriarchy, extreme hierarchy and centralization, it seems likely that the church's present increased tolerance is due as much to changes in society as to changes in the institutional church.

If the institutional church had been more influenced by a Catholic liberal tradition in relation to values and structure, the evils of which the institutional church has been guilty might never have occurred. If the institutional church had been more influenced by notions of a Catholic liberal psychology, such as the church having duties and obligations in regard to individuals rather than only rights, then Catholic history would have been more Christian. If there had been a greater presence in the institutional church of women, or more particularly of the values that mostly have been held by women, then the history of the church would be less characterized by intolerance and violence done to others. If the institutional church had been influenced less by a debased ethic of justice and more by the ethic of care associated with women, then Catholic history would have been more characterized by love, care and compassion.

Within the institutional church women, while acknowledging the value of the justice ethic when not debased by authoritarianism, patriarchy and extreme hierarchy, need to retain an ethic of care and a concern for the individual; and they would need to move men more in the direction of the same values. In *Answer to Job*, Jung anticipates, almost in terms of a divine advent, a future development that will make us more fully human and whole. Jung seemed to see in the dogma of the Assumption intimations of a feminine principle about to give birth to such a change. He described the church's 1950 proclamation of the bodily Assumption of Mary into heaven as the most important religious event since the Reformation. Jung saw the dogma as expressing, psychologically, the need for the feminine not only to be represented in the Godhead, but also to be incorporated into human personality. Perhaps Jung is also anticipating here what he would have regarded as a psychological advance: an incorporation into the church of values which historically have for the most part been those of women, and the elevation of women to equal status with men in the structure of the institutional Catholic Church.

8

Existential Selfs and God

Who is it that can tell me who I am?

(Shakespeare, *King Lear*)

There is something uncreated and divine in the soul.

(Meister Eckhart, *Defence*)

God is the sole good. All the goods contained in things have their equivalent in God.

(Simone Weil, *Gateway to God*)

A competent biography about, say, an eminent artist tells us a great deal about her. The biographer begins by examining the influence of innate factors and early psychological experience. We learn about the family she was born into, and that both her parents were active and dynamic. We read about the outgoing fun-loving mother and the witty but reserved father. The biographer relates that at an early age the future artist seemed to have inherited her mother's lively extraversion and at school displayed her father's dry humour.

The biographer adds to our understanding by reporting the father's difficulty in expressing affection for his talented daughter, the occasional conflict within the family, the parents' neglect of their seemingly self-sufficient girl when a frail younger brother was born. In the light of modern psychology, no one could doubt the crucial importance of these early experiences. The biographer develops the picture by reporting the social circumstances of the young artist – her family's lower-middle class status, the snobbishness of the provincial town where she grew up, art college where she no longer felt an outsider, the influence of her friends and acquaintances at home and later at college. Then we read of her subsequent artistic achievements. By the time the biography ends, we have some understanding of her personality and life.

But we might put down the book feeling something is missing; the artist remains a puzzle in spite of the biographer's painstaking account. The biographer has failed to penetrate to the heart of her mystery as a person. Why did she develop her art in a particular direction? Why did she choose to leave her husband – if it really was a choice? Why did she live where she did? What about her un-explained depressions and the seemingly distant relationship with her children? What did she really think about in those last years of her life? Hamlet complains to Rosencrantz and Guildenstern that 'you would pluck out the heart of my mystery', but this would seem to be the very thing that the biographer has failed to do.

Existential psychology originates from existentialism, a philoso-phy which starts from the conscious experience of human beings; existentialism affirms that since the experience of each of us is unique, every individual – our artist included – remains ultimately a mystery. Emphasizing the uniqueness of each individual and of every individual's experience, existential psychology regards the whole person as a problem for a scientific psychology.

Existential psychology acknowledges the value of a scientific account of the empirical personality. Science demonstrates cause and effect in human personality; what we think, feel and do is large-ly the product of our biology, past experience and present circum-stances. But existential psychology, while recognizing such forces as inevitably constraining our lives, sees most human beings as some-times in a position to choose. Our occasional free choices, regardless of how coerced and restricted they are, suggest another limitation to the cause-and-effect explanations of science. Existential psych-ology, in affirming the possibility of apparently free and uncaused choices by the existential self, further suggests why the artist, and each of us, is more than can be understood by science.

The existential self or 'I' which, according to existential psych-ology, is the experiencing centre of personality and the source of our limited choices, is also seen as a problem for science. My 'I', when studied by psychology, ceases to be 'I' and becomes a Me. Once the experiencing and subjective 'I' comes, metaphorically, under the microscope, the subjective experience escapes; and the 'I' changes from subject to object. The 'I' or the existential self can never become a target for objective enquiry by ourselves and others, and can never be stood outside of and studied scientifically.

But psychologists and biographers, turning human subjects into objects for the purposes of study, illustrate a danger for all of us. In a human relationship, when we treat the other as an object and as less than a whole person, something crucial in the relationship escapes. Object-relations theory holds that humans seek in their relationships to be acknowledged and experienced as a whole person by another, and to acknowledge and experience that other as a whole person. And when in a close and loving relationship we experience the other person in this way, we become aware – according to existential psychology – of that other as more than just the product of biology, past experience and present circumstances. Existential psychology maintains that in a loving and intimate encounter, we sense in the other person a depth that seems infinite; at the same time we go beyond ourselves.

Whatever the biological buzz of sex without a relationship, as in pornography, masturbation or casual sex, the experience is partly that of encountering limits and peering, like a confined animal, through the bars of a cage. Existential psychology maintains that in a fulfilling human relationship, sexual or non-sexual, when as 'I' or self we experience the other as 'I' or self, as subject and not object, we touch infinity in the other person – and transcend. The 'I' or existential self within another, and ourself, seems endless, infinite and like an ever-receding horizon.

Existential philosophers, such as Karl Jaspers, regard human life as characterized both by this transcending which the existential self occasionally experiences and by the confining experience of empirical existence. Each of us is an existential self, seeking to reach the far side of our confining experience and to move beyond. We are all of us aware within ourselves of a longing to transcend both the empirical world and our own selves; existentialists regard this as part of human experience. They recognize a dimension within personality which attempts to go, and sometimes succeeds in going, beyond empirical existence. And it is not only in human love and deep personal relationships that we transcend or attempt to transcend the constricting empirical world. Existential psychology recognizes our attempts to do so in such areas as artistic experience, scientific study, religious practice. According to existential psychology, the 'I' or existential self attempts by a variety of means to go beyond the material world and transcend.

A Christian existential psychology, like secular existentialism, also regards each human self as unique. God, according to Christian existentialism, does not regard human beings in general terms – such as 'human beings'! – but identifies each of us as a unique person. An emphasis on the uniqueness of each individual and every life means, for existential psychology, that certain kinds of truth are existential. For example, what matters about the truths of religion is how the individual relates to them. What is the point of being convinced intellectually by arguments for the existence of God, if the belief that I achieve with such proofs is detached, cerebral and fails to move me? A Christian existential psychology, emphasizing the personal nature of religious truths, recognizes the need for church dogma to touch the individual.

Christian existentialism sees that church teachings must relate to the human knower and have such significance for the individual that they evoke commitment. The beliefs of Catholicism become wholly meaningful only in the subjective experience of individual Catholics. Christian truths are, in this sense, existential because they affect us only when they become our own personal truths.

Though emphasizing uniqueness, existentialism holds that, besides the longing to transcend, there are other experiences common to human beings; one is an awareness of the fragility of our lives. Existentialism also recognizes a certain contingency as the common experience of human beings, a sense that my life might never have happened. Existential psychology sees that this awareness of the apparent arbitrariness of having been born and being alive, and of the seemingly equal arbitrariness of death, results in a sense that our lives have no meaning. Existential psychology recognizes that an awareness of our fragility, of our contingency and of the seeming meaninglessness of our lives, causes other existential experiences, such as anxiety, guilt, despair. Such experiences are existential because they are simply a consequence of being an existing human person, and so inevitable.

Each of us has everyday anxieties, some of which might be helped by therapy, but existential psychology recognizes a radical anxiety existing beneath them all: we are worried about not existing; we dread the non-existence that permeates our being; we are afraid of our contingency and of not-being. Existential psychology sees us as anxious about our nothingness because we are aware how close our 'to be' is to 'not to be'. There is no escaping such anxiety, which has nothing to do with poor toilet-training or sexual repression, but is caused by our awareness of death, and which exists as part of our very self.

Existential psychology also regards guilt and despair as inevitable, and largely a consequence of the failure to fulfil our potential. Damaging experiences when young as a result, for example, of clumsy parenting or Catholic attitudes to sex, can cause guilt or despair which therapy might help. But existential psychology sees that there exists an existential guilt and despair, which result from our almost inevitable failure to become our true self. Such a view resembles the liberal Catholic perception of sin as a failure to become the person that God created me to be. Though our empirical personality is largely the product of biology, past experience and present circumstances, existential psychology holds that an authentic self is something to be achieved; and to the extent that we are unsuccessful in becoming our true self, to that extent we despair.

Existential psychology recognizes that attempting to become our true self involves change, and change involves risk. In seeking our true self we might, like Oedipus, discover something about ourselves we would prefer not to know. We could brace ourselves against change and choose to stay as we are, but existential psychology maintains that refusing the attempt to achieve our true self causes guilt; each of us feels guilt to the extent that we refuse to change, grow and move in the direction of our full potential and true self.

The experiences that existential psychology describes are frequently referred to in Thérèse's autobiography. Thérèse always prayed that she would see things as they really are; at times this moved her to an existential realization of a void in her life and of a closeness to not existing. She writes of an awareness of her own nothingness and of a fog that at one time engulfed her. This fog became so dense, and for a long time so completely enveloped her, that she no longer had any sense of a future happiness with God. While the fog lasted she could see death only as bringing her to a 'night of nothingness'.¹ But she asserts that in this fog and this 'night of nothingness', God is – though not experienced by us.

For atheistic existentialism, a sense of our own nothingness confronting an existential void confirms the irrelevance and absurdity of life. But for Thérèse the confrontation is between the abyss of our self and the abyss of God. She holds that an awareness of our own nothingness relates us immediately to the Absolute Being of God who is and who is infinite Love. For Thérèse, the awareness of our own nothingness ceases to be a cause of anxiety since such an awareness moves us in the direction of our need for God. We are helpless, we are nothing even, but God is an abyss to which we can trustingly abandon ourselves. So Thérèse does not despair, because she sees God as holding her nothingness in being, which makes her safe enough.

Thérèse sees the cross saying to Christians that negative experiences such as anxiety, guilt, despair, suffering and failure are an inextricable part of life. She comments, in her autobiography, 'my consolation is to have none on earth'.² Thérèse makes us aware that we can capitalize on these negative experiences by transforming them into opportunities to allow ourselves to fall into the hands of a God who loves us. God's supposed claims on justice, insisted on by a nun in Thérèse's presence and strongly emphasized by the Catholic authoritarian tradition, occupy a minor position in Thérèse's scheme of things. And she sees any such claims as having already been met by Christ on the cross. Any guilt on our part is immediately confronted by God's merciful love. For Thérèse, no evil exists which God's compassion cannot get rid of; this makes irrelevant the anxiety, guilt and despair which Thérèse sees as threatening to alienate us from God. She recognizes that such alienation can only be ended by turning to the one God that exists, the

God of love. And Thérèse sees that God regards each of us with a love which invokes in us a reciprocal love.

For Thérèse, negative experiences like anxiety, guilt, despair, suffering and failure enable us to accept the reality of not being in control of our lives. She sees such experiences as helping us abandon ourselves to this compassionate God. She writes in her autobiography of having at a particular time 'great interior trials of all kinds, even to the point of asking myself whether heaven really existed'.[3] As a result of her own experience, she is under no illusion that this abandonment to God will necessarily fill our lives with consoling religious experiences. Elsewhere in *Story of a Soul* she says: 'When I sing of the happiness of heaven and of the eternal possession of God, I feel no joy in this, for I sing simply what I WANT TO BELIEVE. It is true that at times a very small ray of the sun comes to illumine my darkness, and then the trial ceases for *an instant*, but afterward the memory of this ray, instead of causing me joy, makes my darkness even more dense.'[4]

Thérèse saw within human personality an ineradicable hope for something better, for a happiness and good for ourselves and others. But she saw also that such hope is inevitably frustrated in life. We experience a chasm between what we want, Freud's pleasure principle, and what we actually get, Freud's reality principle, and realizing that the chasm is unbridgeable we despair. But Thérèse contends that our despair at not finding happiness here and now leaves us with no alternative but to abandon ourselves to God. And for Thérèse, abandoning and trusting ourselves to this hidden God is enough, since God is both the goal of our lives and the means of achieving the goal.

Psychology demonstrates that we need to be accepted completely and that only when we are completely accepted by others can we become ourselves. Thérèse saw that we need to have our loving acceptance by other people underpinned by God's love. She sees that, no matter how much love we receive from other human beings, God 'alone could fulfil my immense desires'.[5] Thérèse focusses on the unconditional nature of God's love; as with a good therapist, there are no strings attached to God's acceptance of us. In object-relations theory, our need for loving relationships is seen as innate but developed by the experience of being loved. Similarly, Thérèse sees that we love God because it is our nature to do so, but also because we learn from God who loved us first.

In his novel *The Diary of a Country Priest*, George Bernanos describes the day-to-day life of a priest discharging mundane duties in a country parish. His life is tedious, and he receives little encouragement or gratitude from the people around him – or seemingly from God. The priest appears to make little difference to the lives of his parishioners, but he continues without bitterness doing what he can. And though there is emptiness and inner dryness in his everyday life, he never quite gives way to despair. Bernanos seems to be suggesting that the priest, in his attention to the unremitting demands of his parish, and in spite of his occasional closeness to despair, is on the path to God. This, in part, is Thérèse's message.

As death approached, she experienced great desolation. But she had always seen death existentially, not as a future event but as a real possibility in the present. Thérèse stressed that since death and non-being are always within us, humans need to be ready to die in every moment. She saw that for herself, as for everyone, even in the absence of consolation, in spite of fear and even of temptations against faith, there needs to be an acceptance of death. For Thérèse, there remains a confidence that the God of merciful love comes with death, though typically she holds that our death will not necessarily be heroic. In her readiness to appear at death with empty hands before God, Thérèse again turns human fragility and contingency into something positive.

In spite of the rules of the church and her Order, Thérèse retains an independence of thought; and after a great struggle she becomes her authentic self. In spite of the circumstances of her mother's early death and her father's breakdown, her lack of education, her powerless situation as a woman, her ignorance of life outside the convent, the constricting convent atmosphere, an authoritarian church which repressed women, she survives. Thérèse demonstrates how it is possible to triumph even in psychologically crushing circumstances and, by courage and embracing the will of God, to emerge a saint. She converts the anger and resentment that she and most of us feel in powerless circumstances, not just into an acceptance, which would be achievement enough, but into a love of God, others and herself.

Thérèse says that she had once been unable to believe there really were people who had no faith; she had found unbelievable the possibility of denying the existence of heaven. She had believed that people who denied the reality of heaven were really speaking against their own 'inner convictions'.[6] But there seemed to be a change, partly related to her own existential experiences of religious doubt. Christ, she says, enabled her to recognize that it is possible for people to have no faith.

Simone, too, saw the anxiety and despair in life, which she attributes partly to the absence of anything good enough in the world for human beings. She regards the absence from human life of anything truly satisfying as something that each of us knows from experience. 'The soul only knows for certain that it is hungry' (*Waiting on God*).[7] Our experience tells us that nothing in the world will satisfy us, says Simone, and our experience is right. She maintains that we only have to be honest with ourselves to recognize that any present or future good in our lives, however wonderful, such as human love, pleasure in the world's beauty or enjoyment of the arts, is never quite enough. 'We all know that there is no true good here below, that everything which appears to be good in this world is finite, limited, wears out and, once worn out, leaves necessity exposed in all its nakedness' (*Waiting on God*).[8] Simone stresses the importance of discarding the illusion that anything in the world will prove enough for us; once we are aware of our dissatisfaction, we search for the possibility of a good existing beyond the world which would satisfy us completely.

Each of us begins life concerned only with our existence in the visible world. But Simone recognizes, in an existential way, that when we become aware how empty the universe is and how little of matter is alive, we realize our insignificance. This awareness of our own insignificance and of the universe's indifference, together with the unfulfilling nature of what life has to offer, loosens our grip on the material world. She maintains that when we relinquish our attachment to the world and discard illusions about happiness in our present existence, a good beyond the world enters us and enables us to accept life. That good beyond the world we call God.

We gradually become aware through our lives, according to Simone, that any absolute good that we long for is not to be experienced within the material world. But she holds that if we direct our attention and love to a good beyond the world, the good eventually comes to us in some limited fashion. And Simone holds that we are all able to receive this good from a reality beyond space and time because each of us is connected with this reality. This good beyond the material world of space and time is God.

Simone is aware that, for most of us, God is conspicuously absent from the natural world. Like Gerard Manley Hopkins in his poem *Nondum*, Simone is disturbed by God's apparent absence. But she regards the experience of God's hiddenness, like our dissatisfaction with life, as valuable. Simone sees God forgoing an obvious presence so that nothing in the world will satisfy us. We only become aware of our need and desire for God in a world where God is absent. And, according to Simone, when we eventually realize that what we have been longing for all the time is God, we recognize that this God exists outside the world and our condition is one of exile. She sees God remaining seemingly absent also in order that there is no obvious satisfaction or pay-off from loving God; God wants our love to be given freely.

But Simone affirms that beneath the surface of an indifferent and unsatisfying universe, God remains secretly present and is to be found and loved. She holds that in love of neighbour, of religious ceremonies, of friends, and of the world's beauty and order, even in the love of this beauty and order expressed in arts and science, we love God, implicitly and indirectly – though we may not be aware of this. She sees these implicit loves preparing us for an explicit love of God; she says that we even implicitly experience God in these four loves. And Simone maintains that if we consistently pay attention and give our love to where the divine is most certainly present, namely, in these four loves, God comes to us and may eventually be experienced by us more directly. And when God comes to us in a more direct and explicit way, other people and the universe's beauty and friends and the rites of religion do not become less valuable to us; on the contrary, says Simone, direct experience of God makes them more real and more precious to us than ever before.

Simone, like Thérèse, recognizes in an existential way the fragility of our existence; but she maintains that when God enters us, we become real and achieve true being. But to enable God to enter, we have first to make ourselves empty by discarding all the accretions and activities with which we try to fill ourselves. She contends that if we leave empty spaces within us and wait, God eventually enters the gaps, emptinesses and desert places in our lives. But Simone adds that to become aware of God, solitude is often necessary. Characteristically, she asserts that each of us is often tempted to evade solitude by escaping into the social; but being permanently fused into a collectivity, such as family, church or any 'us', can operate as an obstacle to God. She holds that, if God is to enter, sometimes one has to be alone.

Simone sees that suffering, such as great pain, personal distress, the despair in our lives, all of which she refers to as affliction, is an important means by which we are emptied. Such affliction, when it just happens and is not chosen, makes us feel abandoned not only by other human beings but also by God. She regards the inevitable and existential experiences of affliction such as despair, guilt and anxiety as ways to God. For Simone, it is by continuing to love what is good, even in times of affliction, that we come to know God. She sees that for the Christian, affliction is a sharing in Christ's experience, especially his suffering on the cross. If we refuse to become bitter, cynical or full of hate when we are afflicted, but instead remain loving and open, we become more like Christ.

Simone Weil does not seem to regard finding or believing in God to be totally under our control. She says in *Gateway to God*: 'It is not for man to seek, or even to believe in, God. He has only to refuse his love to everything which is not God. This refusal does not presuppose any belief.'⁹ We merely acknowledge what we already know, says Simone, that nothing in the world satisfies us, and then wait. A collection of her writings is titled, significantly, *Waiting for God*. Simone's concern with 'waiting', with a belief that something important will come, resembles the religious feel in Samuel

Beckett's play, *Waiting for Godot*, where the tramps cling to the hope that Godot will eventually arrive. Simone contends that after great waiting, when we might not even know what we are waiting for, God enters, if only for an instant.

And when, consequent on our waiting, God enters in some way or becomes present in the waiting, this often happens secretly and unknown to us. No deep religious experience might be involved, and we might remain very aware of the natural world's apparent indifference and of the dissatisfaction that the world generates within us. But, says Simone, if we can believe that, beneath the universe's indifference and our discontent, the truth about reality is love, then we have found faith. For Simone, faith is believing that the reality of the world is love and that this reality is a loving God.

Like Simone Weil, Catherine sees that the soul longs for what is good and she is told by God in the *Dialogue*: 'You cannot arrive at virtue except through knowing yourself and knowing me.'[10] She sees this knowledge of self and of God acquired in what she calls a 'cell of self-knowledge'.[11] Catherine holds that each of us needs some inner space, a cell within, where we can learn about God and ourself. She sees that part of what we acquire in this cell of self-knowledge is an awareness of our inclination to sin and an appreciation of our own nothingness. In the *Dialogue*, God describes sin very existentially as 'nothingness'[12] and 'the opposite of being';[13] and Catherine's words and thoughts often express an existential awareness of our closeness to not existing. She asserts that within the cell we come to appreciate the absoluteness of God's existence, which contrasts with our own fragile hold on being. In the *Dialogue* she addresses God: 'Thus I see that you are who you are, infinite eternal Good, and we are the ones who are not.'[14]

Catherine maintains that the appreciation of our self's nothingness and inclination to sin, acquired in the cell of self-knowledge, serves to make us humble. But she holds that if we are too preoccupied with our self, and insufficiently mindful of God's goodness and love, we despair. When within the cell we arrive at a knowledge of God's compassion and love for us, there is no danger of despair. But Catherine holds that if we concern ourselves exclusively with God's love for us, there is a danger of pride and presumption; this is why the humility which comes from knowing our own self is so important. According to Catherine, when we balance our sinfulness and nothingness against the reality of God's love, we achieve not only humility but also a security in God that frees us from anxiety, guilt, despair.

Catherine's notion that in the cell of self-knowledge we balance our sinfulness against God's love resembles the Jungian integration of shadow into conscious personality. In Jungian psychology, increasing our knowledge of our own shadow is like reclaiming and draining land from the sea. With such reclamation from the sea of the unconscious, we become aware of the irrational, childish, aggressive, raw sexual, greedy, power-obsessed shadow side of ourselves. But shadow, once reclaimed from the unconscious and made conscious, becomes an area of potential growth. According to Jungian psychology, as the conscious self accepts and integrates more shadow, the individual moves towards becoming a more whole and individuated person. In a similar way, in Catherine's account, our sinful inclinations need to be redeemed within the cell of self-knowledge by the presence of God's love. She reports that in the cell of self-knowledge we come to value ourselves, knowing our worth as created in God's image and as destined to be united with God in eternal life.

Modern psychotherapy stresses the importance of felt experience for self-knowledge. Similarly, Catherine holds it to be through experience of our self and God that we arrive at a knowledge of our own identity and God's reality. She sees knowledge of self and knowledge of God as linked; true self-knowledge comes only when we see ourselves in relation to God. We learn to know ourselves, who we are and what we are, by looking at God. She uses the image of a mirror to illustrate how we arrive at a true understanding of ourselves when we see ourselves as God sees us. Looking 'in the gentle mirror of God',[15] says Catherine, what we realize is that through no merit of ours we have been made by God in God's own image. 'And if anyone should ask me what this soul is,' God tells her in the *Dialogue*, 'I would say: She is another me, made so by the union of love.'[16]

Catherine holds that just as we come to know ourselves better by knowing God more, so the realization that our self is made in God's image increases our knowledge of God and, specifically, of how good God is to us. According to Catherine, our love of God and of other people grows as our knowledge of God increases in the cell; as our love of God and others increases, so too does our knowledge of God and others. For Catherine, love and knowledge relate, and the way to God is through an interplay between love and seeking the truth.

Though Catherine holds that God's truth is one, she stresses that truth comes in a variety of ways to different human beings. A Christian psychology sees individual differences, as in our personalities, innate make-up, psychological experience and social situations, as relating to the variety of ways in which God's truth comes to different human beings. God says about people in the *Dialogue*: 'The eye cannot see, nor the tongue tell, nor can the heart imagine how many paths and methods I have, solely for love and to lead them back to grace so that my truth may be realized in them!'[17] And our motivation for this truth and love is, of course, the motivation to find and experience God. Human beings, God tells Catherine, were created by Love and were created with such a capacity for love that they cannot live without love. Without the uncreated Love that made them they will never be satisfied. 'Only I can satisfy you,'[18] God tells her.

Julian, similarly, states in the *Revelations*: 'Lack of the joy we were created to have fills us with deep desire.'[19] She sees the central motive of our life to be the search for God. And, like existential psychology, she notes the restless and unsatisfied quality of human life: 'This place is a prison, and this life is penance.'[20] But Julian holds that, if we seek God, an element of 'the joy we were created to have' can be experienced here and now. We find joy in our present life to the extent that we experience God's love directly and in other people, and also in the anticipation of the enjoyment of God in eternal life.

Julian concluded from what God had revealed to her that because we are human, sin is inevitable – in modern terms, existential. But she expresses a horror of sin and stresses the pain and damage that we cause others and ourselves by sinning; and aware of the resulting shame and guilt, she speaks of sin as making us repulsive to ourselves. She says that for love's sake we should, as God does, hate sin which caused Christ's suffering; but she stresses that we should, as God does, love sinners, ourselves included. She holds that sin never puts us beyond divine love and compassion; God is always with us, loving and forgiving, regardless of what we do. But though Julian regards God's compassion and forgiveness as total and immediate, she sees that sin can prove an obstacle to our finding God and to our moving to become one with God. To sin is to do what harms other human beings and potentially prevents us growing to God and our true self.

But, like many psychologists, Julian regards people as excessively prone to guilt and to blaming themselves. Many of us, experiencing existential guilt, find that the stories of Kafka touch a nerve because, like his central characters, we are dismayed by the excessive feelings of guilt that we sometimes find within ourselves. But Julian, since she sees God as never judging, encourages us to feel less guilty and to value ourselves in spite of any real or imagined wrongdoing of ours. She learns from God to regard our wrongdoing as opportunities to learn about ourselves and for psychological growth. Like a psychotherapist, she values self-knowledge and sees sin as enabling us to acquire insight into ourselves. For Julian, sin – like neurosis in Jungian psychology – negatively reveals our potential. In Camus' novel *The Fall*, the complacency of the judge–penitent is destroyed by remorse and guilt, but only to be replaced by cynical self-deprecation. For Julian, a recognition of our own sinfulness should, by reducing our egoism, result positively in our becoming more compassionate and less judgmental of others – and ourselves.

Julian holds that sin, by demonstrating our frailty and how dependent we are on God, makes us open ourselves humbly to God. Indeed, she contends that when sin makes us aware of our inadequacy, causing us to feel guilt, anxiety and despair, we are especially able to recognize that what matters is God's love and compassion. Sin, in Julian's account, is potentially able to make us more truly human and further our growth to God. In the *Revelations* she understands that God, especially as a result of Christ's redemption, can bring something good from the damage and harm done by sin. At times Julian sees sin more as a sickness; and she declares that the cure for this sin-sickness, and related guilt, is to be found in knowing God's love.

She disapproves of fear in our relationship with God, particularly of a 'doubting fear' which 'draws us towards despair'.[21] This 'doubting fear', referred to by Julian, seems to be a lack of trust manifesting itself in anxiety and obsessive concern with doing our duty. There is only one fear which Julian finds pleasing to God, a 'reverent fear',[22] which she sees as having much in common with love and is, perhaps, better described as 'awe'. Julian regards any other fear as without justification and likely to obstruct our relationship with God, which she regards as helped by an absence of fear. Julian continually stresses that the divine hatred of sin never stops God loving the sinner, and she records in the *Revelations* that she sees no anger or blame in God.

Modern psychotherapists emphasize the importance of achieving an awareness of who we are, and Julian, too, stresses the need to discover our true identity. In the *Revelations of Divine Love*, she stresses the mystery of the human self and asserts that our self is profoundly involved in the being of God. Julian's emphasis on a relationship between discovering our self and discovering God is akin to Jung's suggestion that if we find the God within we might find the God without. She contends that we cannot really know God till we know our own self, and we can never really know our own self till we know God. And she suggests, almost impertinently, that in our present life it is harder to know ourself than to know God. But Julian promises in the *Revelations* that in God's presence 'we shall see and know, truly and clearly, what our self is – when we see our God, truly and clearly, in the fullness of joy'.[23] When we see God after death, we will really understand this self of ours, so mysterious in life.

The existential emphasis on the mystery of self contrasts with reductionist psychology's view that a complete explanation of personality is eventually possible. A reductionist psychology anticipates a day when no further study is needed because the text books will contain a comprehensive account of personality. In contrast, existential psychology holds that people cannot be totally understood by analysing and reducing down their unique selfs. Existential psychology further contends that each of us is more than we can know even about ourselves. All of us are more than the sum of our parts. Existentialist psychologists also observe that when we attempt to understand another person, our experience is of seeming never to reach a final boundary within that person. Existential psychologists also observe that even in the experience of ourselves, we seem never to become aware of an ultimate boundary. If our artist had written an autobiography, we would still not understand her completely – nor would she. At the end of our lives, all of us, our artist included, remain a mystery to others – and ourselves.

Both a secular and Christian existentialism regard the human person as ultimately unknowable – by science or ourselves. The attempt to know others or ourself encounters an ever-receding horizon. And each existential self is unknowable not because of the limited nature of our knowledge but because the human self seems without limits. A Christian existential psychology, believing every human being to be made in God's image, regards the mysterious-ness of the self as a consequence of a divine dimension to person-ality. A Christian existential psychology sees this divine element as enabling the existential self to achieve its occasional triumphs over the cause and effect of the natural world and, sometimes, to go beyond the material world.

Influenced by existentialism, Karl Rahner, the twentieth-century Catholic philosopher and theologian, characterizes the human being as one who goes beyond; for Rahner, the person is a transcending being whose experience does not come to rest in the world. But wherever our transcending ends, Rahner and most existentialists recognize that the material world is where our experience and transcending begins. Uplifted by a popular tune, but knowing that life never fulfils the promise of music . . . enjoying conversation in a public house with friends, but conscious the evening is passing . . . in a deep human love, where we experience seemingly infinite depths in the other person and ourselves . . . praying in a church at dusk, at peace but sad . . . in a supermarket or at work, when we acknowledge the dissatisfaction within us . . . in these and other moments we go beyond the material world and transcend. In such moments – of the everyday, or of artistic, scientific or religious experience, or of sexual love or any deep personal relationship – we become aware of an emptiness and hunger within; but in such moments our self seems also to go beyond and touch something that would fill our emptiness and satisfy.

A Christian existential psychology recognizes that such moments, whether of dissatisfaction at work, of the experience of the depth within another person, of transient enjoyment within the pub, make us recognize how unsatisfied we are; but they also appear to hint at some fulfilment. We have a sense of great happiness just eluding us. Julian seems similarly to be suggesting an awareness of a happiness glimpsed when she says in the *Revelations*, 'Lack of the joy we were created to have fills us with deep desire.'[24] In the restlessness at the supermarket, in the mixed pleasure of the tune, in the profound love of another, we not only experience our hunger and dissatisfaction but we seem almost to touch whatever eludes us. In such moments, we not only long to go beyond our earthly experience to something more satisfying but appear actually to do so. How could we experience our life as inadequate and unfulfilling, unless we have already experienced something better?

In such moments the self often seems to transcend and become aware of . . . something longed-for beyond. There is restlessness and discontent in these experiences, but we touch something fulfilling; they not only express our desire for happiness but seem also to contain a brief experience of what would make us happy. Such moments fill us with longing and a sense of separation but also, for an instant, satisfy as they tap into a longing which exists within the self. The power of such experiences arises not from the revelation of a lost childhood utopia but as a glimpse of a not-as-yet discovered paradise. Such experiences, by putting us in touch with our longing, connect us for a moment with the object of that longing, namely, God.

God, Existential Selfs and the Church

To see a World in a Grain of Sand
And a Heaven in a Wild Flower,
Hold Infinity in the palm of your hand
And Eternity in an hour.

(William Blake, 'Auguries of Innocence')

This conception of a looser relation on the part of the individual Christian to
the teaching of the official Church does not lead out of the Church nor does it
place us on the fringes.

(Karl Rahner and Karl-Heinz Weger, *Our Christian Faith*)

'I am infinite Good and I therefore require of you infinite desire.'

(God addressing Catherine, *Dialogue*)

Returning hill-walkers, pausing for a moment, stare down and see
the ridge immediately below them. When they descend further,
another ridge becomes visible. As they continue their descent, ridge
after ridge is revealed, with every succeeding ridge encompassing a
previous ridge as the hill broadens to the plain below. In the same
way, and as with our knowledge of our inner existential self, so too
our perception of the external world never seems to arrive at an
awareness of a final boundary. The mind's attempt to grasp outer
reality confronts a succession of horizons, each horizon encompassing the previous horizon and contained in a subsequent horizon.
When we think about the external world, we are met by horizons
that recede infinitely; and our mind is unable to know external
reality in its entirety.

Existential philosophers, such as Karl Jaspers, see common sense
and science as explaining objects in the outer world. But they maintain that commonsense thinking and science cannot explain and

understand the external reality containing these objects. Every time our minds attempt to grasp outer reality like a final horizon, and just as we seem about to know the external world complete and entire, another horizon rises. When we appear to have grasped reality as an all-encompassing horizon, we have only created another limited horizon which is no longer the horizon that contains all horizons.

The hill-walkers know they will eventually descend the last ridge to the plain below. But Jaspers and other existentialists recognize that our mind, in studying external reality, never passes a penultimate horizon to arrive, like the hill-walkers, at an all-encompassing plain. Like the inner existential selfs of ourself and others, external reality never becomes an object that we can totally know. The whole world never fits the straitjacket of our concepts; the ultimate outer reality that we are looking for is always below the horizon.

From early on, Christian thinkers were aware of the problem in relation to the divine; we say that God is indescribable, and in doing so we *describe* the *indescribable* God. When we give God a label or description, God ceases to be the ultimate and all-encompassing reality that we are seeking. In Christian theology this led to a 'negative way'; Eckhart, the medieval mystic and theologian, says, 'That which we say is God, God is not.' Both a secular and Christian existentialism recognize that no definitive account of ultimate external reality is possible.

Though we never capture with our concepts this horizon outside us which contains all horizons, we feel that such a horizon exists. Karl Jaspers uses the term 'transcendence' to describe this ultimate horizon which contains the specific horizons of external reality, but which is never seen and not situated within other horizons. An existential psychology contends that when we reach the boundaries of commonsense exploration of the whole of outer reality, and when, in scientific thinking about the totality of the world, we arrive at the limits of our knowledge, we seem to go beyond boundaries and limits to experience this horizon-below-the-horizon, we seemingly experience an external transcendence. Religion, the arts, philosophy and theology attempt to express this transcendence.

In conventionally religious situations, such as praying in church, people sometimes find themselves reaching out and appearing to touch this transcendence outside us. For many, secular contexts like art galleries or the countryside provide experiences of an external transcendence. Whether the context is religious or secular, the existential self arriving at an awareness of limits and boundaries appears to become aware of something beyond the material world. At such limits or boundaries, the self seems to experience the horizon-below-the-horizon. In a moment of quiet within a church, of awe before a Rembrandt painting, of wonder at a sunset, each of us is aware of this external transcendence that we cannot capture with our minds. Such experiences appear to mediate for the existential self an awareness of an external presence beyond thought.

The religious believer believes that this presence is God. In the fifteenth century Nicholas of Cusa, a Christian theologian, writes of the human mind encountering a boundary in its search for God. He describes this boundary as a wall between the world's finite objects and an encompassing God the far side of the wall. We cannot penetrate the wall, but in the encounter and our attempt to break through we sense, says Nicholas, the God beyond.

Modern Christian existentialism, too, regards this experience of a transcendence not reducible to an object in the material world, but remaining always beyond, as the experience of God. Karl Rahner refers to the experience of mystery. But this transcendence or mystery, containing all external reality, remains God only as long as we avoid reducing it to an object of thought. Once we have supposedly grasped the all-encompassing God in our thinking, what our thinking now holds can no longer be God. Athanasius expressed this early in the Christian era: 'God does not exist; God is not an object; and only objects exist.'

But Jaspers' existentialism, and Rahner's specifically Christian existentialism, maintain that when our mind fails in the attempt at complete conceptual knowledge of the world, something of value emerges. Such existentialism holds that in the seeking and not finding, each of us approaches, comes close to and sometimes even encounters this presence the far side of Cusa's wall. In the failure of our minds searching for understanding, we touch, at the limits of our knowing, the mysterious and ultimate horizon beyond words and thought. In a search never achieving comprehensive knowledge, we occasionally experience transcendence. For the existentialist, the 'negative way' is not entirely negative.

Jaspers asserts that what we sometimes experience, when our objective exploration of outer reality ends in not-knowing, is a consciousness of God. And a consciousness characterized by not-knowing would seem an appropriate awareness of a transcendent God. For most of us, any other sort of consciousness would be of an object into which our thinking had turned God. The value of the conceptual not-knowing of external reality, where our search eventually arrives, is an awareness of a God beyond knowledge. A religious existentialism holds that in our encounter with the limits and boundaries of thinking about the entire world, we occasionally transcend and actually experience a divine presence.

Stepping out into the night and gazing up at the dark sky, the stars make us gasp with wonder. The sight of the stars heightens a longing within us and a sense of loss. But the experience of longing and loss suggests that we have actually experienced what we long for and appear to have lost. We return from such moments feeling that the ordinariness of the everyday is not enough. And we realize, perhaps not consciously, that in such moments we must actually have experienced that something better which makes the everyday inadequate.

A Christian existential psychology holds that though at one level we fail in our thinking and knowing and worship to go beyond Cusa's wall, at another level we succeed. Though the horizon-below-the-horizon, transcendence or mystery sensed in the night sky remain beyond objective knowledge, they touch something in us. The moment passes. But we continue to stare up at the stars, look at pictures in art galleries, attend concerts, just as we once walked on pilgrimages, searching for the horizon-below-the-horizon, transcendence and mystery, external to us as well as within, which we traditionally call God.

Christian existential psychology sees, as Julian does in the *Revelations of Divine Love*, the search for God as a central motive of our lives. Christian existential psychology holds our search for God to be motivated by an absence and a presence. We are often aware of the seeming absence of Isaiah's 'hidden God'. But Christian existential psychology also affirms a presence; according to a Christian existentialism, we are moved and motivated by a presence of God that we might not consciously recognize, but which we experience when we look at the stars or at pictures in an art gallery.

According to secular existential psychology, the self's motivation to go beyond the limits of everything objective, and to move towards the all-encompassing horizon, originates within us. Christian existential psychology similarly regards the source of our striving, to breach Cusa's wall and go beyond to God, as located in the individual. Simone Weil writes in *Gateway to God* that, 'at the centre of the human heart, is the longing for an absolute good, a longing which is always there and is never appeased by any object in this world'.[1] Existential psychology would hold that Simone's words express what can hardly be denied, since they simply capture our experience. But Simone Weil goes further, as does Christian existentialism, to suggest the existence of an external reality corresponding to our longing for absolute goodness. For an existential Christian psychology and for Simone, this reality is, of course, God. In *Waiting on God* she says: 'All that man vainly desires here below is perfectly realized in God. We have all those impossible desires within us as a mark of our destination.'[2]

Existential psychology, though stressing that this search for something beyond is motivated from the self, recognizes that any such search is invariably made within a social context. For most of us, the search, though ultimately personal, needs a specific location such as the arts, a religious tradition, or academic studies like philosophy or physics. And though our ultimate goal may be the horizon-below-the-horizon, transcendence, mystery, God, since we are human and have bodies, our search begins from what is concrete and specific: the symbols and beauties of the arts, the concepts and truths of psychology or physics, the practices and beliefs of religion.

For Roman Catholics, a central context for the search is the church, and part of the search of Catholics for God is made through the symbols, beliefs and ceremonies of Catholicism. A religious existential psychology recognizes that humans are social beings and usually need a community within which to seek God. Karl Rahner recognized the value for Catholics of tradition, authority and revelation within the church; he saw untrammelled openness, and complete freedom for the individual, as ending in anarchy. But Rahner was aware that the greater danger, in the Catholic Church, was a totalitarianism which suppresses freedom and free enquiry.

Similarly, Karl Jaspers' existentialism sees the search for truth and God conducted between two extremes of unconditional faith and total openness. The extreme of unconditional faith, which Jaspers significantly terms Catholicity, exists where a tradition regards its account of truth as definitive, universal, absolute and unchanging. The Catholic authoritarian tradition, which holds church dogma and rules concerning God and the human person to be objective and final, is an example of unconditional faith. Jaspers, while rejecting the unconditional faith of Catholicity, does not support the alternative extreme of total openness. He points to the dangers in total openness of obscure vagueness, of everything being too problematic and of all views being excessively conditional.

For the Catholic liberal personality, commitment to openness is balanced by an appreciation of an informed and enlightened understanding of revelation, tradition and church authority. The Catholic liberal personality, like existential psychology, recognizes that even total openness to reason fails to provide complete enlightenment. But Jaspers regards a certain openness as an essential component of faith. And Jaspers values an open faith between the two extremes of unconditional faith and total openness. He holds that a willingness to accept risk and uncertainty and change, characteristic of an open faith, is essential in the search for truth and transcendence. Similarly, the Catholic liberal personality sees that openness with an acceptance of uncertainty and the possibility of change are essential though painful elements in the search for God and truth. The Catholic liberal tradition and a Christian existential psychology recognize that the search for God is balanced and enriched within the context of the church, but both regard the search as ultimately individual and personal.

The uniqueness of every individual and of every individual's search is emphasized by Thérèse; she stresses the variety of paths by which God leads different people. She is existentialist in her emphasis on the primacy of the individual self's relationship to

God. In her own life, freeing herself from excessive preoccupation with the rules of church, religious order and convent, she is guided by her own inner experience of Christ. 'I understand and I know from experience that: "*The kingdom of God is within you.*" Jesus has no need of books or teachers to instruct souls; He teaches without the noise of words.'[3] Thérèse's life and thought are characterized by confidence in her own religious experience; for the most part she decides for herself what to do. Like a modern psychologist, Thérèse sees that excessive emphasis on unreflecting obedience to authority prevents people becoming fully human and capable of love. An existential Christian psychology holds that believing solely on the basis of the authority of the institutional church usually proves inadequate and – in contrast to personal faith – is not even a spiritual act.

Thérèse stresses our need to be mature independent adults, able to love; she anticipates modern psychology in her awareness that we need to be a free and independent self to be capable of loving relationships. Thérèse is clear that we can love God and others, and abandon ourselves to God, only if we go beyond being merely the product of conformity and obedience. Indeed, only if we go beyond mere conformity and obedience to become independent human beings, do we really have a self.

Like Thérèse, Catherine also values the church but stresses time and again in the *Dialogue* the importance of the relationship between the self and God. Catherine, again as with Thérèse and the Catholic liberal tradition, also emphasizes the personal nature of the search for love and truth which brings us to God. The God of love is to be found in our neighbour, who is everywhere; and God tells Catherine not to 'want to force all my servants to walk by the same path you yourself follow, for this would be contrary to the teaching given you by my Truth'.[4] Throughout the *Dialogue*, the individual's personal relationship with God is emphasized, and Catherine sees that ultimately all have to find their own path to God.

Similarly, Simone Weil saw the danger for Catholics of acquiescing in a Roman Catholic collectivity and of remaining dependent, in an immature way, on certain institutional features of the church. For example, numbers of Catholics, usually those in the authori-

tarian tradition, appear fixated on a celibate clergy, extreme hierarchy in church structure and an authoritarian papacy. Simone
holds that for people to develop, both as human beings and as
Christians, a kind of liberation is eventually necessary. She also
recognizes a danger, particularly for those brought up as Catholics,
of becoming so insulated in church membership that we stop
growing psychologically. Simone adopts an existentialist emphasis
in holding that Catholics, even as members of the church, have to
follow their own path to God. And an existential Christian psychology recognizes that following one's path to God might involve for
the Catholic, after much reflection and thought, ignoring certain
rules preached by the contemporary church of her or his time.
While Simone saw that church teaching often enabled the individual to come to a knowledge of God, she recognized that most
Catholics needed to develop a certain independence, intellectual
and emotional, from the church.

Fairbairn's object-relations theory sees human development in
terms of a growth from infantile to mature dependence. Such
development requires achieving a balance between dependence
and independence in adult relationships. For Roman Catholics,
infantile dependence in our relationship with the church is characterized by identifying ourselves completely with the institutional
church; the self has little or no separation from the church, and
individuals regard themselves largely in terms of 'being a Catholic'.
The object-relations account would see that such Catholics, in order
to achieve psychological growth and become adult Christians, have
to leave the womb of mother church. But achieving adult personality as a Catholic does not involve a severing of relationships with
the church.

Achieving the security of the adult personality requires, in object-
relations terms, moving from infantile dependency on 'mother'
church to an interdependence characterized as mature dependence
based in adult relationships. Such mature interdependence is
typically indicated by a certain separation from the church of the
individual and the individual's identity. The Catholic, no longer
psychologically fused with the institution, is able to relate to the
church appropriately. Such a relationship would be based on a

realistic appreciation of the church rather than on an infantile 'my mother is a saint' idealization, which obstructs the individual's psychological growth. And in an adult relationship of mature inter-dependence, where the self is capable of mature relationships while retaining a certain autonomy, the individual gives to, as well as receives from, the church. At the very least, what most Catholics would be able to give to the church is their own felt experience of life, their individual search for God and questioning, and their own personally experienced answers.

Less reliance on the institutional church, and more on one's self, seem psychologically desirable; but many Catholic social com-mentators suggest also that it is simply becoming necessary. The religious faith of Catholics living within secular society now has less and less support socially; so the faith of the individual Catholic is more likely to survive if she or he has acquired a personal faith which is not so dependent on the institution of the church.

Simone Weil, asserting the primacy of the individual self, was particularly aware of the dangers of conformity and excessive dependence in institutions. She sees individual humans, and not social institutions, as ends in themselves; she regards the value of an institution as always relative. In contrast, Catholic teaching, even into the early twentieth century, seemed to continue identifying the institutional church with God's kingdom on earth; such a view was consistent with Catholic authoritarian tradition's belief, held for nearly fifteen hundred years, of 'No salvation outside the church', and which popes had proclaimed as church doctrine from the early thirteenth century. But even conservative Roman Catholic thought now acknowledges that only a universal kingdom of God, and not the institutional church, is of absolute value. Rahner and Weger implicitly recognize that the church is not an end in itself when they refer to 'the hope that one day the eternal kingdom of love will exist and not the church' (*Our Christian Faith*). The realization that eventually the church will cease to exist, and that God's universal kingdom alone will endure, makes clear that the value of the church is relative and that only the value of all human beings is absolute.

But even Catholics dismayed by the church's history of violence done to others, and by the preoccupation of popes and the institutional church with power, are aware that the basis of their own faith is owed partly to the continuation of the church as an organization. Such Catholics value membership of a community of ordinary people who, in an attempt to give meaning and wholeness to their lives, seek God. What many Catholics experience as of particular value is the presence of Christ, the mass, the sacraments, the New Testament, devotion to Mary, and the search for God in the thought and mystical tradition of the church. Such Catholics value the church as a community of lay people, nuns and priests, existing in a network of caring relationships.

But a tension exists for many Catholics between a need for the church and for the freedom that the unique individual requires in the search for God and wholeness. Such tension is greatly increased by authoritarian church structures and by values such as patriarchy, often the cause of church intolerance and persecution of others in the past, and which remain largely unchanged in the present. But Simone Weil recognized the potentiality of the church as a community and, stating an ideal, she says in *Waiting on God*: 'The incarnation of Christianity implies a harmonious solution of the problem of the relations between the individual and the collective.'[5] But she quickly qualifies this by stressing, as the condition for such harmony, the freedom of thought which she always considered central: 'This harmony exists wherever the intelligence, remaining in its place, can be exercised without hindrance and can reach the complete fulfilment of its function.'[6]

Essential for such harmony is an adoption, by the institutional church, of existential psychology's and the four women's emphasis on the primacy and absolute value of each human self. The Christian liberal tradition has always stressed the uniqueness of every human self and has seen God as concerned with the individual; Christianity expresses this in the assertion of God's love for each human being. The tension between the organization and the individual would be less in an institutional Catholic church which regarded its own function largely as serving each and every person.

Nevertheless, the Catholic liberal tradition acknowledges a polarity between the requirements of the institutional church and the needs of the individual Catholic seeking God and truth. Rahner holds that a tension between the church and the individual is inevitable and that consequent conflict has constantly to be negotiated. Catholic liberal tradition regards this dialectic in the church, between the institution and the individual Catholic seeking God, as not only inevitable but desirable, achieving a never final, but always moving, balance.

The four women's concern for every individual relates to the ethic of care which all four stress. Thérèse's God, for example, is characterized by a non-judgmental compassion for all; and Thérèse regards the true Christian as characterized by a concern for each person, expressed in a loving relationship. And though, in Catherine's *Dialogue*, a rule-bound God judging according to a debased justice ethic is sometimes present, he seems the projection of a despotic fourteenth-century church. For the most part, Catherine's God is compassionately concerned for everyone and wants all human beings to care for each other. God tells her in the *Dialogue*: 'In this mortal life, so long as you are pilgrims, I have bound you with the chain of charity.'[7] Catherine sees that, for the Christian, the belief that God became human and died on the cross reveals God's love and compassion for every human being. And Julian, troubled by the church's judgment that we are sometimes sinners deserving of anger and blame, emphasizes God's unconditional love. An ethic of care constantly emerges in Julian's report that God desires a relationship with each of us.

Simone Weil too emphasizes the love and compassion for the individual which characterizes an ethic of care; but she particularly stresses that our concern should not be limited to those close to us. The Catholic liberal tradition, similarly, in contrast to the authoritarian tradition's excessive and narrow allegiance to the institutional church, embraces the whole human family. Christ gives as an answer to the question 'Who is my neighbour?' the story of a passer-by helping a complete stranger. While Simone Weil recognized in the Good Samaritan the value of a love and compassion that is specific and at the same time implicitly universal, she contrasts this with a love and caring that is explicitly universal. Simone felt that the modern day required our love of others explicitly to embrace everyone. She says in *Waiting on God*: 'We are living in times which have no precedent, and in our present situation universality, which could formerly be implicit, has to be fully explicit.'[8] She is advocating here a universal caring ethic with compassion, care and love for each person; the neighbour that we are to love is everyone and everywhere.

Within Catholicism, an ethic of care is likely to increase and flourish more when the institutional church ceases to be authoritarian, patriarchal and excessively hierarchical. Psychology suggests that for this to happen democratization of the institutional church is necessary. Jean Piaget observed psychological growth and development in children. As a consequence of his research, Piaget came to see moral development in terms of a move from a heteronomous to an autonomous stage. In the first (heteronomous) stage, morality is regarded by the individual as being subject to and abiding by the laws of others; such laws are externally imposed by an authority like parents, school, government, pope. In the second (autonomous) stage, morality is regarded by the individual in more democratic terms; here morality is regarded largely in terms of accepting and abiding by rules agreed between equals. Piaget sees the move from a heteronomous to an autonomous stage as a significant moral advance; similarly, the Catholic liberal personality and tradition value moving from the papacy as a sole source of authority within Catholicism to a more democratic form of church authority.

Thompson (1990) sees expressed in the writings of Thérèse, and especially in her notion of the Little Way, an affirmation of what he calls a Catholic form of the 'democratic principle'. Thérèse stresses in her autobiography the richness of the lives of ordinary individuals: 'I understood, too, that Our Lord's love is revealed as perfectly in the most simple soul who resists His grace in nothing as in the most excellent soul.'[9] In an essay on Thérèse, Thompson maintains that her thought is relevant not only to individual people but more broadly to the whole church. Thérèse, stressing the dignity of every individual, and seeing each of us as uniquely loved by God, asserts a sort of priesthood of the people. And Thompson regards Thérèse's assertion of the value of ordinary people as what he terms 'a "Catholic" form of the Protestant priesthood of all believers, a radical critique of all ecclesial elitism'. Thompson suggests that this democratic principle has significant ramifications for the 'magisterial' function of the church. With such a democratic principle, authority is seen to be located in all members of the church; the Catholic liberal tradition affirms such a view.

For the Catholic liberal personality and tradition, the implement-ation of a democratic principle, and a democratization involving structural change, both locating authority in all members of the church, would be significant moral development. Among such possible changes are: involvement of lay women and men in the selection and appointment of priests; involvement of diocesan priests and representatives of laity in the election of bishops; greater devolution of authority to regional hierarchies; all bishops to be involved in the election of a pope, with the pope subsequently accountable to bishops' representatives; the Roman Curia to be replaced by staff having an administrative function only; bishops to meet regularly in General Councils, with the pope as bishop of Rome participating as 'first among equals'; formal teaching authority to reside in general councils of the church.

Thérèse's Little Way can be seen as an implicit criticism of an elitism and a hierarchy of power within the Catholic Church. Her perception leads away from a hierarchical top-down church to a more democratic structure. Thérèse affirms the value of what we all experience in our ordinary daily lives; she maintains that, since each of us is guided by God, our need for multiple directives from the church is limited. Simone Weil may never have become a Catholic, but the thought and lives of all four women would seem to demon-strate that the individual can search for God even in the context of an authoritarian, patriarchal and excessively hierarchical church, and in doing so help to improve institutional church values. The individual Catholic's constant search for God and truth prevents church authority, tradition and interpretations of revelation from hardening into irrelevance. Liberal tradition recognizes that, in the Catholic Church, the beginnings of renewal usually originate in the experience of ordinary priests and people.

Influenced by the Catholic liberal tradition and by an existential psychology, a more democratic church would value equality and freedom above an extreme emphasis on obedience and compliance to its own authority. A Catholicism inspired by an ethic of care, and by the liberal tradition, would affirm a love that embraces all human beings above unbalanced allegiance to the church. Within such a Catholicism, love for the individual would take precedence over concern for the institutional church. Such a caring and liberal church would be motivated more by the institution's obligations to others than by any sense of the church's own rights. A caring and liberal church, influenced by a Christian existential psychology, would exist primarily to give worth to unique individual lives.

A crucial insight of the ethic of care and of existential psychology is that true understanding of another human being requires experiental knowledge of that person. Both a caring ethic and a Christian existential psychology recognize the need to start from the reality of where people are. Understanding of where a particular person is requires specific knowledge of that individual, such as the uniqueness of his or her biology, of the person's past psychological experience and of present social circumstances. A caring, liberal and existential church places concern for the individual above an excessive preoccupation with church rules; such a church acknowledges, as did Thérèse, 'how different are the ways through which the Lord leads souls!'[10]

And a church motivated by a caring ethic would subordinate a judgmental preoccupation with rules and principles to compassion and concern for the individual. Significantly, in an ethic of care, general moral rules and principles that do exist are invariably about relationships; and a reading of the New Testament confirms Christ's teaching to be concerned with relationships. A general rule involved in an ethic of care is that we ought to care for others. A general and absolute principle underpinning the caring ethic is that everyone has a right to be cared for – including the carer. 'Compassion,' reflects Prince Myshkin in Dostoyevsky's *The Idiot*, 'was the most important and, perhaps, the only law of human existence.'

The Catholic liberal tradition, while stressing the primacy of the individual's search for God, recognizes that such a search usually needs the context of a religious community, and that for a Catholic this is the church. Freud held that social institutions should do for human beings what instincts do for animals, direct behaviour along appropriate channels. And Simone Weil believed that the church as an organization can guide our search for the divine along appropriate paths. She saw the ceremonies of the church as helping Catholics to see all created beings related to each other and God. But Simone, seeing the world sacramentally and God present in all creation, held that love of neighbour, friendship, love of the beauty and order of universe, were important mediators of God's grace, independent of any institutional church.

Roman Catholics are sometimes tempted to stop believing in the existence of a God in whose name the institutional church has persecuted, tortured and killed so many human beings. But, like the atheist in a Dostoyevsky novel who complains that God has tormented him all his life, for many of us it might not even be possible to stop believing in a God. Our existential selfs are constantly haunted by a horizon-below-the-horizon and transcendence, and by a mystery which will not leave us alone.

Two such selfs, both women, stand in an art gallery deeply moved before a Rembrandt painting. The vulnerability of Rembrandt's wife in the painting and the haunting luminosity of the image of her everyday world evoke in them a deep sense of mystery. The women feel as if the boundaries of their selfs are extended; they experience the picture as seeming to connect them to something more than themselves. One woman reflects: 'What I feel here is the experience of God.' The other, who rarely thinks in religious terms, reflects on the power of art. What the first woman has described as an experience of God, the other has labelled an aesthetic experience. A Christian existential psychology regards as correct the 'experience of God' label.

But a Christian existential psychology holds that the experience is more important than the correct label. Christian existential psychology holds that having the experience is more valuable than using religious dogma to label what we have experienced as God. Jung even maintains that if we are obsessed with using dogma to provide a religious label, possibly to shore up uncertainty about our Christian belief, we are less likely to have the experience.

But whatever the label that we give to such experiences, their reality cannot be denied. The source of such experiences may be a Rembrandt painting, loving and being loved by another person, an awareness of the horizon-below-the-horizon in the material world, the feeling at work or in the supermarket that life is not enough, a moment of stillness in church, our failure to grasp the universe whole and entire, the good tune that moves but leaves us unsatisfied, awe at the marvel of relativity theory, a sense of infinite depth in oneself and the selfs of other people. Existential psychology stresses the reality and value of these experiences, which seem to relate us to something larger than ourselves.

And the view of Christian existential psychology that having the experience is more valuable than attaching the 'experience of God' label reduces the importance of distinguishing between secular and sacred, non-religious and religious, non-believers and believers. Julian of Norwich often makes little distinction in her *Revelations* between the secular and the sacred: 'The fullness of joy is to see God in all things.'[11] Julian is aware of God's closeness to everyone and of how we grow to God in our everyday secular existence. Catherine too sees love and the search for truth as taking us to God. Her *Dialogue* holds that the God of love is to be found in loving our neighbour and the God of truth is to be discovered by a variety of paths.

Simone Weil particularly disliked the division of people into believers and non-believers. While she recognized the love of God implicit in the believer's love of religious ceremonies, she saw that for many people, especially in modern times, religion meant little. Simone held that, in the lives of those without belief, the love of God implicit in friendship, love of neighbour and love of the world's beauty compensated for the absence of formal religion. She disliked how in the past the institutional church had denied the presence of God among atheists and agnostics. She especially disliked the church's reluctance to recognize, in the fortitude of atheists and agnostics facing suffering and affliction, an implicit acceptance of God's will.

The four women and secular psychology stress the centrality of human relationships for our development to personal wholeness. But the four women also emphasize that our self requires the confirmation of its identity in a relationship with God. 'If we want to know our soul, and to walk and talk with it,' says Julian, 'it is absolutely necessary for us to reach into our Lord God, in whom it is enclosed.'[12] Catherine too sees a connection between the reality of God and an appreciation of our own true identity. Catherine holds that, through experience in the cell of self-knowledge, we come to a realization of the reality of God and of God's love for us, crucial to an awareness of who and what we are. A Christian existentialist psychology too regards a relationship with the horizon-below-the-horizon or transcendence, which is God, as essential in achieving our true self.

Julian, emphasizing this interrelation between God and the self in the *Revelations*, stresses our one-ness with God: 'And I saw no difference between God and our substance but, as it were, all God. And yet my understanding took it that our substance is contained within God.'[13] But Julian maintains that though in this union we are contained within God, we do not fuse with God in such a way as to lose our identity. Our self's participation in God's being is such, according to Julian, that we retain our identity while finding ourselves completely in the interpersonal intimacy of a relationship with God.

Christian psychology sees the existential self as seeking a God who is the transcendent horizon-below-the-horizon but remains God only when not reduced to an object of knowledge. A Christian psychology holds also that human beings too are unattainable horizons, transcendence, mysteries that objective science cannot ultimately explain. Christian existential psychology sees God's revelation in Christ as reducing, but not dispelling, the essential mystery not only of God but also of our own self and the selfs of others.

A Christian psychology recognizes the existence within every human self of an element which relates to the divine. The identity and wholeness that we achieve through social, sexual and personal relationships with other human beings are central and crucial for us, but not enough. We crave that which alone could satisfy us, an infinite God who draws us on . . . infinitely. A wholly secular psychology regards such 'infinite' longing as pathological. But a

Christian psychology declares such longing to originate in the reality of a human need which can only be satisfied by a God who is both external and within the self. Our eternal happiness will consist in the relationship of our self with God; after death we will experience more fully the mystery of God; and in God's presence we will more completely relate to and experience the mysterious selfs of other human beings. But that is not yet; our situation for the present remains largely one of anxiety, uncertainty and longing.

But Christian existentialist psychology asserts that even now, whether or not recognized by us, the experience of the horizon-below-the-horizon in great art, of a mystery which disturbs us as we stare at the stars, of transcendence felt in deeply loving and being loved by another human being, is God's presence. And we are not only moved by receding horizons, mysteries and transcendence external to us, but also by experience of the mysterious self which each of us is; we are moved by the experience of a mysterious presence within our self and the selfs of others, which too is the presence of God. And though the experience is more important than the label, a Christian existential psychology holds that knowing the correct label is of value; the correct label is the experience of God, and knowing this confirms that our human loves are underpinned by a Divine Love.

Secular psychology explains much about us, but certain dimensions in our lives seem beyond science and objective knowledge. A Christian psychology and the four women see our lives as grounded in a hope and meaning given to them by what we traditionally call God. In the end, we are confronted in our experience by a Mystery which constantly calls us back to belief, and by a Horizon that infinitely recedes but seems sometimes a longed-for and loving Presence.

Notes

Details of most quotations from the four women are given below. Julian quotations are from *All Shall be Well*, a version of *Revelations of Divine Love*, abridged, arranged for daily reading and translated into modern English by Sheila Upjohn, published by Darton, Longman and Todd 1992; page numbers below refer to this version. Quotations from Catherine's *Dialogue* are from the Suzanne Noffke translation, published by Paulist Press 1980; page numbers refer to this publication. Quotations from Thérèse's *Story of a Soul* are from the translation by John Clarke, published by ICS Publications 1996; page and chapter numbers refer to this publication. Quotations from Simone Weil are from: *Waiting on God*, translated by Emma Craufurd, page numbers refer to the Collins Fount Paperbacks 1977 reprint of the Routledge publication; *Gateway to God*, edited by David Raper, page numbers refer to the Collins Fontana Books 1974 publication; *Gravity and Grace*, translated by Emma Craufurd, page numbers refer to the Ark Paperbacks 1987 imprint edition of the Routledge paperback. Details on these texts are given in Sources.

Introduction

Introductory Julian quotation, *Revelations of Divine Love*, Ch.56, p.123.
1. *Revelations of Divine Love*, Ch.63, p.145.

1. God Made in Our Image

Introductory Julian quotation, *Revelations of Divine Love*, Ch.56, p.124.
1. *Dialogue*, Ch.133, p.272.
2. *Dialogue*, Ch.159, p.344.
3. *Revelations of Divine Love*, Ch.85, p.190.
4. *Dialogue*, Ch.31, p.72.
5. *Story of a Soul*, Ch.4, p.84.

2. *But for the Grace of God and . . .*

Introductory Julian quotation, *Revelations of Divine Love*, Ch.76, p.173.

Introductory Catherine quotation, *Dialogue*, Ch.100, p.191.

1. *Waiting on God*, p.174, Concerning the 'Our Father'.
2. *Gravity and Grace*, p.1, Gravity and Grace.
3. *Story of a Soul*, Ch.8, p.180.
4. *Dialogue*, Ch.100, p.191.
5. *Dialogue*, Ch.100, p.191.
6. *Dialogue*, Ch.98, p.185.
7. *Revelations of Divine Love*, Ch.76, p.173.
8. *Revelations of Divine Love*, Ch.27, p.44.
9. *Revelations of Divine Love*, Ch.82, p.185.
10. *Revelations of Divine Love*, Ch.45, p.87.
11. *Revelations of Divine Love*, Ch.27, p.44.
12. *Revelations of Divine Love*, Ch.82, p.185.

3. *The Psychology of Two Catholic Personalities*

Introductory Julian quotation, *Revelations of Divine Love*, Ch.86, p.192.

1. *Dialogue*, Ch.44, p.89.
2. *Dialogue*, Ch.44, p.89.
3. *Revelations of Divine Love*, Ch.56, p.123.
4. *Revelations of Divine Love*, Ch.56, p.123.
5. *Story of a Soul*, Ch.9, p.200.
6. *Dialogue*, Ch.11, p.44.
7. *Dialogue*, Ch.7, p.38.
8. *Story of a Soul*, Ch.9, p.195.
9. *Revelations of Divine Love*, Ch.86, p.192.

4. *The Psychology of Two Catholic Traditions*

Introductory Simone Weil quotation, *Waiting on God*, p.46, Letter 4, Spiritual Autobiography.

1. *Dialogue*, Ch.104, p.197.
2. *Gateway to God*, p.115, Letter to a Priest.
3. *Revelations of Divine Love*, Ch.11, p.18.
4. *Waiting on God*, p.47, Letter 4, Spiritual Autobiography.

5. *Psychological Growth*

Introductory Julian quotation, *Revelations of Divine Love*, Ch.58, p.132.

1. *Dialogue*, Ch.104, p.196.
2. *Revelations of Divine Love*, Ch.28, p.46.
3. *Story of a Soul*, Ch.11, p.246.
4. *Revelations of Divine Love*, Ch.61, p.140.
5. *Revelations of Divine Love*, Ch.40, p.70.

6. *Catholic Patriarchy*

Introductory Julian quotation, *Revelations of Divine Love*, Ch.59, p.133.
Introductory Thérèse quotation, *Story of a Soul*, Ch.9, p.192.

7. *The Institutional Church*

Introductory Simone Weil quotation, *Waiting on God*, p.21, Letter 2, Hesitations Concerning Baptism.

1. *Gravity and Grace*, p.148, The Great Beast.
2. *Gravity and Grace*, p.145, The Great Beast.
3. *Waiting on God*, p.46, Letter 4, Spiritual Autobiography.
4. *Gravity and Grace*, p.146, The Great Beast.
5. *Dialogue*, Ch.134, p.273.
6. *Story of a Soul*, Ch.9, p.194.
7. *Waiting on God*, p.97, Forms of the Implicit Love of God.
8. *Story of a Soul*, Ch.8, p.180.
9. *Revelations of Divine Love*, Ch.45, p.88.
10. *Dialogue*, Ch.103, p.195.
11. *Story of a Soul*, Ch.9, p.188.

8. *Existential Selfs and God*

Introductory Simone Weil quotation, *Gateway to God*, p.41, Selected Pensées.

1. *Story of a Soul*, Ch.10, p.213.
2. *Story of a Soul*, Ch.9, p.187.
3. *Story of a Soul*, Ch.8, p.173.
4. *Story of a Soul*, Ch.10, p.214.
5. *Story of a Soul*, Ch.8, p.175.
6. *Story of a Soul*, Ch.10, p.211.
7. *Waiting on God*, pp.161–2, Forms of the Implicit Love of God.

8. *Waiting on God*, p.162, Forms of the Implicit Love of God.
9. *Gateway to God*, p.85, Some reflections on the Love of God.
10. *Dialogue*, Ch.43, p.88.
11. *Dialogue*, Ch.1, p.25.
12. *Dialogue*, Ch.35, p.76.
13. *Dialogue*, Ch.31, p.73.
14. *Dialogue*, Ch.134, p.274.
15. *Dialogue*, Ch.13, p.48.
16. *Dialogue*, Ch.96, p.181.
17. *Dialogue*, Ch.4, p.31.
18. *Dialogue*, Ch.48, p.98.
19. *Revelations*, Ch.42, p.81.
20. *Revelations*, Ch.77, p.175.
21. *Revelations*, Ch.74, p.166.
22. *Revelations*, Ch.74, p.166.
23. *Revelations*, Ch.46, p.89.
24. *Revelations*, Ch.42, p.81.

9. God, Existential Selfs and the Church

Introductory Catherine quotation, *Dialogue*, Ch.104, p.197.
1. *Gateway to God*, p.38, Selected Pensées.
2. *Waiting on God*, p.85, The Love of God and Affliction.
3. *Story of a Soul*, Ch.8, p.179.
4. *Dialogue*, Ch.104, p.196.
5. *Waiting on God*, p.43, Letter 4, Spiritual Autobiography.
6. *Waiting on God*, p.44, Letter 4, Spiritual Autobiography.
7. *Dialogue*, Ch.148, p.311.
8. *Waiting on God*, p.62, Letter 6, Last Thoughts.
9. *Story of a Soul*, Ch.1, p.14.
10. *Story of a Soul*, Ch.10, p.207.
11. *Revelations of Divine Love*, Ch.35, p.58.
12. *Revelations of Divine Love*, Ch.56, p.123.
13. *Revelations of Divine Love*, Ch.54, p.118.

Sources

The following are the important sources used throughout the book. References specifically cited in the text are listed as well as works whose ideas have influenced the writing of this book.

Abbott, W.M. (ed.), *The Documents of Vatican II*, London: Geoffrey Chapman 1966

Adorno, T.W., Frenkel-Brunswik, E., Levinson, D.J., and Sanford, R.N., *The Authoritarian Personality*, New York: Harper and Row 1950

Allen, Diogenes, *Three Outsiders: Pascal, Kierkegaard, Simone Weil*, Cambridge, MA: Cowley Publications 1983

Banton, M., *Roles*, London: Tavistock 1965

Barrett, William, *Irrational Man*, London: Heinemann 1961

Boswell, John, *Christianity, Social Tolerance, and Homosexuality: Gay People in Western Europe from the Beginning of the Christian Era to the Fourteenth Century*, Chicago: University of Chicago Press 1980

——, *The Marriage of Likeness: Same-Sex Unions in Pre-Modern Europe*, London: Fontana Press 1995

Bro, Bernard, *The Little Way. The Spirituality of Thérèse of Lisieux*, London: Darton, Longman and Todd 1997

Carey, Terence (ed.), *Thérèse of Lisieux, A Discovery of Love, Selected Spiritual Writings*, New York: New City Press 1992

Carlen, Claudia (ed.), *The Papal Encyclicals*, Vol.4, 1903–1939, A Consortium Book, Wilmington, NC: McGrath Publishing Co 1981

Catechism of the Catholic Church, Libreria Editrice Vaticana, London: Geoffrey Chapman 1994

Catherine of Siena, *The Dialogue*, translated and introduced by Suzanne Noffke, OP, New York: Paulist Press 1980

Chodorow, Nancy, *The Reproduction of Mothering*, Berkeley: University of California Press 1978

Clement, Grace, *Care, Autonomy, and Justice: Feminism and the Ethic of Care*, Oxford: Westview Press 1996

Conn, Joann Wolski, 'A Feminist View of Thérèse', in *Experiencing Saint Thérèse Today*, Carmelite Studies 5, ed. John Sullivan, Washington, DC: ICS Publications 1990

de Rosa, Peter, *Vicars of Christ. The Dark Side of the Papacy*, London: Corgi Books 1993

Durka, Gloria, *Praying with Julian of Norwich*, Winona, MN: Saint Mary's Press 1989

Erikson, E.H., *Childhood and Society*, New York: W.W.Norton ²1963

——, *Identity and the Life Cycle*, Psychological Issues, Monograph1,1, New York: International Universities Press 1959

Fairbairn, W.R.D., *Psychoanalytic Studies of the Personality*, London: Tavistock/Routledge 1952

Falconi, Carlo, *The Popes in the Twentieth Century*, London: Weidenfeld and Nicholson 1967

Farrell, Melvin L., *Getting to Know the Bible. An Introduction to Sacred Scripture for Catholics*, Milwaukee, WI: HI-TIME Publishing Corp 1984

Fatula, Mary Ann, *Catherine of Siena's Way*, London: Darton, Longman and Todd 1987

Freud, Sigmund, 'Some Psychical Consequences of the Anatomical Distinction Between the Sexes', *Complete Works*, Vol.19, London: Hogarth Press 1925

——, New Introductory Lectures on Psycho-Analysis, *Complete Works*, Vol.22, London: Hogarth Press 1933

——, An Outline of Psycho-Analysis, *Complete Works*, Vol.23, London: Hogarth Press 1940

Fromm, Erich, *The Fear of Freedom*, London: Routledge and Kegan Paul 1942

——, *Psychoanalysis and Religion*, New Haven: Yale University Press 1950

——, *Man for Himself*, London: Routledge and Kegan Paul 1956

——, *The Sane Society*, London: Routledge and Kegan Paul 1956

——, *To Have or To Be?*, London: Jonathan Cape 1976

Furlong, Monica, *Thérèse of Lisieux*, London: Virago Press 1987

Grotstein, James S., and Rinsley, Donald B. (ed.), *Fairbairn and the Origins of Object Relations*, London: Free Association Books 1994

Hall, C. S., Lindzey, G., Loehlin, J. C., and Manosevitz, M., *Introduction to Theories of Personality*, New York: John Wiley & Sons 1985

Hopcke, Robert H., Carrington, Karin Lofthus, and Wirth, Scott (eds), *Same-Sex Love and the Path to Wholeness*, Boston, Massachusetts: Shambhala Publications 1993

Jacobi, Jolande, *The Way of Individuation, The Indispensable Key to Understanding Jungian Psychology*, New York: Meridian, New American Library 1983

Jaspers, Karl, *Way to Wisdom*, New Haven: Yale University Press 1954

——, *Philosophy of Existence*, Oxford: Blackwell 1971

Johnson, Vernon, *Spiritual Childhood A Study of St Teresa's Teaching*, London: Sheed and Ward 1977

Julian of Norwich, *All Shall Be Well: Revelations of Divine Love*, abridged and arranged for daily reading by Sheila Upjohn, London: Darton, Longman and Todd 1992

Jung, C.G., 'Stages of Life', in *The Structure and Dynamics of the Psyche: Collected Works*, Vol.8, London: Routledge and Kegan Paul 1960

——, 'Psychology and Religion', 'Brother Klaus', 'Psychotherapists or the Clergy', 'Answer to Job', in *Psychology and Religion: Collected Works*, Vol.11, London: Routledge and Kegan Paul 1958

——, 'Introduction to the Religious and Psychological Problems of Alchemy', in *Psychology and Alchemy: Collected Works*, Vol.12, London: Routledge and Kegan Paul 1953

——, *Letters, Vol.2*, selected and edited by Gerhard Adler in collaboration with Aniela Jaffé, London: Routledge and Kegan Paul 1976

Kegan, Robert, *The Evolving Self: Problem and Process in Human Development*, Cambridge, Mass. and London: Harvard University Press 1982

Küng, Hans, *Christianity. Its Essence and History*, London: SCM Press 1995

Lewis, C.S., *The Abolition of Man*, London: Fount Paperbacks 1978

McNeill, John J., *The Church and the Homosexual*, London: Darton, Longman and Todd 1977

Maslow, Abraham H., *Toward a Psychology of Being*, New York: Van Nostrand Reinhold, ²1968

May, Rollo (ed.), *Existential Psychology*, New York: Random House, ²1969

Mead, George Herbert, *Mind, Self and Society*, Chicago: University of Chicago Press 1934

Miles, Siân (ed.), *Simone Weil: An Anthology*, London: Virago Press 1986

Milgram, Stanley, *Obedience to Authority*, London: Tavistock Publications 1974

Moore, Gareth, *The Body in Context: Sex and Catholicism*, London: SCM Press 1992

Mountney, John Michael, *Julian of Norwich, Sin Shall Be a Glory*, London: Darton, Longman and Todd 1992

Noddings, Nel, *Caring, A Feminine Approach to Ethics and Moral Education*, Berkeley: University of California Press 1984

O'Collins, Gerald, *The Second Journey: Spiritual Awareness and the Mid-Life Crisis*, Dublin: Villa Books 1979

O'Driscoll, Mary (ed.), *Catherine of Siena – Passion for the Truth, Compassion for Humanity: Selected Spiritual Writings*, New York: New City Press 1993

Pelphrey, Brant, *Christ our Mother. Julian of Norwich*, London: Darton, Longman and Todd 1989

Piaget, Jean, *The Moral Judgment of the Child*, London: Routledge and Kegan Paul 1932

Rahner, Karl, *Christian at the Crossroads*, London: Burns and Oates 1975

——, and Weger, Karl-Heinz, *Our Christian Faith*, London: Burns and Oates 1980

Rees, Richard, *Simone Weil: A Sketch for a Portrait*, London: Oxford University Press 1966

Rhode, Deborah L. (ed.), *Theoretical Perspectives on Sexual Difference*, New Haven: Yale University Press 1990

Rogers, Carl, *On Becoming a Person*, London: Constable 1961

Rokeach, M., *The Open and Closed Mind*, New York: Basic Books 1960

Schilpp, Paul Arthur (ed.), *The Philosophy of Karl Jaspers*, La Salle, Illinois: Open Court Publishing Company 1957

Scudder, Vida D. (ed. and trans.), *Saint Catherine of Siena as Seen in her Letters*, London: J.M.Dent and Co 1905

Sheppard, Lancelot C. (ed.), Syllabus of the Principal Errors of Our Time 1864, in *Twentieth Century Catholicism*, No 1, a periodic supplement to the *Twentieth Century Encyclopedia of Catholicism*, New York: Hawthorn Books Inc 1965

Six, Jean-François, *Light of the Night, The Last Eighteen Months in the Life of Thérèse of Lisieux*, London: SCM Press 1996

Skinner, B.F., *Beyond Freedom and Dignity*, London: Penguin 1973

Springsted, Eric O., *Simone Weil and the Suffering of Love*, Cambridge, MA: Cowley Publications 1986

Studzinski, Raymond, *Spiritual Direction and Midlife Development*, Chicago: Loyola University Press 1985

Sullivan, Francis A., *Salvation Outside the Church? Tracing the History of the Catholic Response*, London: Geoffrey Chapman 1992

Thérèse of Lisieux, *Story of a Soul, The Autobiography of St. Thérèse of Lisieux*, translated from the Original Manuscripts by John Clarke, OCD, Washington, DC: ICS Publications ³1996

Thompson, William M., 'Thérèse of Lisieux: A challenge for doctrine and theology – forerunner of Vatican III', in *Experiencing Saint Thérèse Today*, Carmelite Studies, ed. John Sullivan, Washington, DC: ICS Publications 1990

Vass, George, *A Theologian in Search of a Philosophy: Understanding Karl Rahner*, Vol.1, London: Sheed & Ward and Westminster, MD: Christian Classics 1985

Weil, Simone, *Waiting on God*, translated by Emma Craufurd, London: Routledge and Kegan Paul 1951, reissued London: Collins, Fount Paperbacks 1977

——, *Gateway to God*, ed. David Raper, London: Collins, Fontana Books 1974

——, *The Need for Roots*, New York: Harper and Row 1976

——, *Gravity and Grace*, translated by Emma Craufurd, Ark Paperbacks, London: Routledge and Kegan Paul 1987

Wilkins, John (ed.), *Understanding* Veritatis Splendor, London: SPCK 1994

Index